LEADERSHIP *in* CHRISTIAN EDUCATION

TEACHING IS AN ESSENTIAL ELEMENT OF LEADERSHIP

AMADI OSONDU

ISBN: 979-8-89031-474-1 (sc)
ISBN: 979-8-89031-475-8 (hc)
ISBN: 979-8-89031-476-5 (e)

One Galleria Blvd., Suite 1900, Metairie, LA 70001
(504) 702-6708
1-888-421-2397

DEDICATION

For Nkechi Beatrice Osondu, my wife and
the first lawyer in the family
&
Anne Chinemerem Oscar-Nliam, my one
and only daughter who gave me
my first grand children.

CONTENTS

ABSTRACT

Christian education is a potpourri of knowledge brewing in church community, stewardship, worship, service, and so forth, and is being harnessed for the purpose of evangelization. Navigating successfully through these windows of opportunity presupposes the existence of sound leadership, which in itself, is a clear demonstration of teaching capability. Teaching thus stands in between the present and the future generation with regard to passing the basic values of life and moral conduct. Consequently, parents and numerous organizations are increasingly seeking a genuine form of education where qualified teachers can be found. In the same vein, there is a brimming challenge to develop a leadership cadre for the future society, and this calls for efforts centered on provision of the right caliber of Christian teachers for the job. It is critical to appreciate that leadership and teaching in Christian education are both meant to focus on man's transformation into the likeness of Christ toward ultimate salvation. Various academic constructs as well as practice outside the Christian educational environment have failed to give prominence to the symbiotic relationship that exists between teaching and leadership.

Recognizing teaching as an element of leadership is necessary for effective and successful results in order to lead anyone back to his Maker. A stand-alone approach has contributed to creating a learning gap, which in turn, has built up a cumulated crisis in the perception and definition of leadership. The dissipation of energy in the process tends to result in unintended consequences. This has led to the restriction of the notion of teaching to a mere passing of knowledge from teacher to learner. The teaching and learning equation is thus skewed in favor of learning to the complete detriment of teaching. The bulk of research in the area/field is concentrated on how to improve learning, and any attempt at shifting focus to teaching becomes limited to simply finding out the quality of institution the teacher in question attended with respect to the pedigree of such institution. The personal qualities of the teacher in relation to knowledge, character, and ability to even teach are simply ignored or are oftentimes regarded as irrelevant.

It thus becomes valuable to understand that in Christian education, there is that subtle marriage of teaching to leadership. The symbiotic relationship lasts throughout life, and those involved in leadership know teaching ends only at the return of Christ who promised He would return, as is the Christian belief it would happen. The unwholesome detachment of teaching from leadership in secular education must be recognized as a deterrent for effectiveness, and there is dire need for further research in reconstruction of the subject to its biblical foundational concept. This will serve the very purpose of leading man back to his Creator with the help of Him who will be with us to the end.

Teaching and leadership is unified by the purpose as provided by God and confirmed in the Scriptures. Disunity creates dissonance, which results in crisis of definition in both terms. Further research in this area will help fix this fundamental error of separating one from the other in order to provide room for better pursuit of a generally acceptable definition of leadership. It will also encourage writers to draw from Christian education principles, which are couched in biblical truth, knowing its inerrancy, notwithstanding the fact that social science principles have been given prominence in human activities even in concepts with their origins in the Bible. We are now looking at one attempt to provide a major pedestal toward efforts at closing the gap and reinforcing the focus of Christ's teaching, which was intentional in the way He trained and equipped His disciples for fruitful service.

AN OVERVIEW

In spite of the overwhelming academic and non-academic work on the separate subject matters of *leadership and teaching*, there is little material combining both as unitary in nature and purpose. This conception is rooted in the definition attributed to each, and where some similarity is perceived, the subsequent exposition tends to contradict the overall goals. Max De Pree, for example, in his effort to define leadership in his work, *The Art of Leadership*, delved straight into what the responsibility of a leader should be, and this theme runs through his argument, which later dovetails into what he considers as qualities of a good leader. The digression of focus from responsibility, which was the starting block, to qualities constitutes a common thread running through most of the available literature on the definition of leadership. This has evidently created a serious gap in the understanding of what a standard definition of leadership should be for use as an appropriate starting point on the subject matter. The immediate effect blurs what really should be seen as the elements of leadership. Other authors like Dr. Tom Dare toed the same line of reasoning and in the process of finding a compromise, instead opened a door for a crisis in definition of the subject.

The crisis becomes glaring when you juxtapose the definitions being propounded with the Christian education concept on both leadership and teaching. Jay Parini, an author, and his counterparts, who see teachers as artistic performers, run substantially in conflict with Christian education perception where it is shown to be a process over the life of both the teacher and the learner. This process turns out to be the uniform string that ties leadership to teaching and vice versa, but is conspicuously lacking in the literature with secular orientation. The crisis of definition stretches from plain understanding that a leader is one who leads a group toward a common purpose to complex analytic comparisons between leading, managing, and directing. The available literature is varied in the perception of the meaning and mostly skewed in favor of the business environment, politics, and other social human activities, but with little attention to what Christian education offers. The crisis is not limited to leadership but extends to the general meaning of teaching as a whole, especially in relation to the biblical meaning at which Christian education propounds both as the foundational and authentic definition. In the midst of the chaos in definition there are only very few writers—like Deborah Chang, R.B. Zuck, Lomenick, and Teach for America (TFA)—who have tried to link teaching with leadership. Rather, both terms are defined to suit situational purposes to fit the writer's design or goal. Authors with a Christian bent admit that all believers are invited and assigned the work of making disciples, with a very clear description of qualities of leaders, and charged with the main goal of passing on the commandments of God to the next generation. The majority of writers on leadership restrict their leadership propositions to whatever narrow window they construct such that leadership in politics is perceived as different from leadership in business, sports, education, religion, and other numerous human endeavors.

This book argues that such compartmentalization enables as well as promotes diversity of goals and justification for creating new purposes, thereby reversing the Christian belief that leadership results in what God wants, that is, God's purpose. It, of course, appears practical and suitable, judging from an ordinary man's reasoning, which shows that the leader determines the purpose and then seeks God's blessing to realize it. All tend to appear to fall in place as the leader can apply his skills and knowledge to amend, alter, or sometimes completely abandon a goal set earlier with any occurrence of change in circumstance or technology. In this frame of reference, leadership success or failure can fairly be evaluated, ignoring the fact that it is predicated on a faulty premise.

Abraham Zelznik leads others like Kutzenmeyer, Marilyn, Jay Parini, Venessa Rodriguez, and others who, by carefully detaching teaching from leadership as if it is a deliberate intention, and projecting them as two separate vocations or professions, constitutes a serious lacuna, harmful to any reasonable effort at having a standard meaning. The unwholesome bifurcation of two essential and integral parts of a vocation as perceived in Christian education justifies the need for a rethink. Some effort has been made to close this gap by the "Teaching as Leadership" group, although it can be argued as simply having broached the subject in the struggle to appease teachers whose image has long been trampled upon.

Purpose is yet another theme in both leadership and teaching, which has been a nagging contention between Christian education and the secular approach to the subject. In order to correct the brewing misunderstanding, further research is absolutely needed. This book hopes to contribute a good measure to this need. A sincere and intimate relationship constitutes a framework for leading and teaching in Christian education, and it is meant to be impactful on those being led in purpose and outcome. Mike Ayers, Lois LeBar, Lawrence Richards, and other Christian education writers agree and insist on the biblical foundation of relating the same to the purpose of transforming the individual in the context of a Christian community where love and personal relationship is featured with prominence. This is seen as similar to the way Christ lived His life while here on earth, imparting Himself and not simply teaching. On the other hand, Barrett, Lomnick, De Pree, Parini, and others interpret *purpose* as the man's personal vision or goals designed for an organization and do not see leadership and teaching in the same light. Their views fall into that typical corporate leadership mesh where a so-called leader would offer the response to a simple question about having room for a new hire with "Oh yes, I can *use* him in the raw-materials handling department!" What seems to matter in this kind of environment is how to exploit whatever capabilities an individual possesses and is not seen as an opportunity to use the talents of the individual while at work to bear the image of God in relation to one another. Intimacy with others or any attachment to godliness does not serve any purpose in order to achieve expected results. By their perception, vision is not dictated by what God wants. A visionary leader in this arena drives the corporate image to new heights.

It is also fair to argue that there exists an inextricable link between *morals and character* these Christian writers refer to when dealing with the subject of leadership. God, who calls His people, is moral, and so the leader must exhibit moral character by honoring God. In this regard, moral qualities define character. Following forthwith, they recognize vision as derived from a "calling," which by itself is imbedded in God's purpose for the leader rather than an invention of the leader. With calling, there must be a Caller whose purpose directs and creates vision as the work progresses, knowing that God is always faithful and would continue to sustain that which He initiates. Leadership in this circumstance considers not only transforming, but with the Christian community, it brews within the relationship formed for growth and edification. In biblical language, vision refers more to prophesying.

There is, therefore, that apparent conflicting usage and understanding, which tends to obfuscate the genuine sense of purpose as to God's purpose in Christian leadership and man's ambition in the business or secular world. Authors seen to have put emphasis on such secular vision reviewed while writing this include Urban Meyer, Albert Mohler, and even the TFA editorial board. While the Christian community operates in the belief that God uses the leader as a vessel through which He gets things done, the secular world portrays a leader as the change agent who works to leave a footprint for generations. Morals, as interpreted in Christian education, are inadvertently replaced with ethics in the secular world, which of course, is often expressed to mean one's conduct in line with professional rules and behavioral standards.

In Christian education, teaching and leadership are not only perceived as wired to have an interlocking relationship but are meant as well to function as a corollary to each other in line with biblical position—the leader must be able to teach! In spite of the discordant notes in defining leadership of the authors reviewed herein, all tend to agree that along with Christian education, every leader needs to be able to ensure continuity. It is my position here that this can surely be accomplished only through the ability to teach even when not explicitly expressed in such language. The obstructing huddle is the failure to recognize the essential position of teaching as an element of leadership, which is my aim to highlight. Ayers, Richards and LeBar all agree completely in their argument that the concept of leadership should be reconfigured to project its biblical foundational meaning in order to capture its comprehensive, moral, and God-oriented perception with a view to preventing or stopping further drift from the truth. Man's quest for variety of purpose in life tends to fuel the passion with which authors and some researchers pursue new thinking, often contradicting the truth, and some Christian writers get carried away by principles developed and seen to work in the social sciences without considering any harmful impact to the Christian community.

It should be of interest to find a good writer like Joseph Nye Jr. agrees with Keith Grint that due to the myriad of variables associated with the topic, it is impossible to arrive at any conclusive definition. The arguments continue to hold in the social sciences that since several variables can be combined to achieve a certain result and since a set of other variables combined would equally obtain a similar result, it renders any definition impossible to predict or determine. Therefore it should be meaningful to state that the indeterminacy has contributed to the disagreement among writers with regard to leadership being categorized as an art or some form of science. As recent as January 15, 2019, *Harvard Business Review* (HBR) released an updated list of what they describe as "Top 25 Best Selling Articles" in which four were featured as leadership specialists written by professors emeriti of Harvard University. Their individual positions remained varied with respect to the main topic being addressed, both in spirit and letter. The article co-authored by Robert Goffee and Gareth Jones, "Why Should Anyone be led by You?" (Sept./Oct. 2000), posits that leadership is predicated on an inherent social relationship of a leader with his followers as regards his ability to meet their needs and expectations. They argue that authentic leaders are skillful at consistently "being themselves' and able to engage the followers' hearts, minds, and souls by being "situation sensors" whereby they can sense goings-on without being explicitly told.

The next article by John Kotter, "What Leaders Really Do" (Dec. 2001), argues that leadership has nothing to do with having charisma or other special personality traits but that leadership and management are two distinctive and complementary systems of action; that while leadership nurtures change, for example, human side acceptance and moving forward, management copes with planning, charting, and organizing, thus dealing with the associated complexity necessary for today's business environment. Following is the article by Jim Collins, "Level 5 Leadership: The Triumph of Humility and Fierce Resolve" (July 2005). This article is said to be based on empirical findings and not on ideological position. Collins argues that effective leaders of the Level 5 cadre, who can transform a company from good to great, should have the common characteristics he discovered in a survey he carried out, namely: humility, will, ferocious resolve, and the tendency to give credit to others while assigning blame to themselves. On whether someone can learn to become a Level 5 leader, he responded positively but with a caveat—under the right circumstance: self-reflection, conscious personal development, a mentor, a great teacher, loving parents, and a significant life experience; and he insists that the latter seems to have sparked their maturation. The fourth and last article under leadership, "Discovering Your Authentic Leadership" (February 2007), was co-authored by Bill George, Peter Sims, Andrew McLean, and Diana Mayer. They posit that the only valid test of a leader is his/her ability to bring people together to achieve sustainable results over time. They went on to emphasize that an authentic leader should demonstrate five traits: pursuing their purpose with passion, practicing solid values, leading with their hearts as well as their heads, establishing connected relationships, and self-discipline. The pivot of their argument lies in their stand that leadership requires years of hard work coupled with the ability to discover the purpose of the leadership.

All four articles share in common the concern for continuation of the group/organization, relationship, knowledge, and above all, a mentor or teacher whose skill will ensure continuity and adherence to the purpose. While John Kotter's concentration is, however, centered on the organization rather than the leader or follower, it does not necessarily oppose the fact that someone has to lead. In summation, three out of the four articles are in support of the call here for rethinking leadership in line with biblical position and recognizing teaching as an essential element of leadership. Kotter simply sidetracked the thesis and may not **certainly** be read as opposing it. I'll rather argue and recommend for a return to the biblical directive where teaching is distinctively positioned as an essential element of leadership—go make disciples ... and teach them—of which Apostle Paul beamed to the Romans as Good News. In the same vein, there is equally the need to rethink the meaning of teaching in order to realign the same to its biblical foundation position with a multifaceted perception and not simply thought of as telling or passing of knowledge. While LeBar and Richards in their separate works put emphasis on this view, Zuck, Parini, and De Pree portray teaching from the familiar and incomplete notion of a classroom activity.

INTRODUCTION

This book is predicated on the understanding that Christian education borders on acquired knowledge, which is far beyond mere "book knowledge." It has its reference to holistic approach to learning with deep interest in spiritual and physical factors in relation to a life process from birth to death. The perfect model is drawn from Jesus's teaching while on earth as recorded in Scriptures and presented in the Bible of which we affirm its inerrancy. The goal of this education is transformational with a purpose as originally designed by the Creator of the universe and man. Our faith in Him as the triune God reflects our belief that Christianity is a faith-revealed religion through special and general revelation as well as experiential exposure to His only begotten Son. This conceptualization can neither be said to be strange nor new, given the fact that it draws from social science theories and is embellished with biblical truth for growth and spiritual maturity.

In this regard, I align my stand about the Bible with this statement by Immanuel Kant: "The existence of the Bible, as a book for the people, is the greatest benefit which the human race has ever experienced. Every attempt to belittle it … is crime against humanity." And following in the same thought is Abraham Lincoln who stated: "I believe the Bible is the best gift God has ever given to man. All the good of the savior of the world is communicated to us through the Book. But for it, we would not know right from wrong." A writer, F. Bettex in 1904, who also reasoned along same line, stated: "Thousands of the best and most talented among men have testified, not only that they never tired of reading and studying it, but also that it constantly grew grander, richer, and more unfathomable." Adding his voice in this direction is Lawrence O. Richards, a well-known authority in Christian education in our present age, who says: "Scripture is true not simply because God spoke it and He is trustworthy. Scripture is true because it accurately reflects the way things are."[1] The Bible, the text I will draw from throughout this book to think about issues of leadership and teaching is the reference authority just as I will argue that it is the root for Christian teaching material source and reference. It is in light of this that we can now engage in the exploration of what teaching in Christian education is meant to portray in a synchronous and seamless unit with leadership.

CHAPTER 1

CHRISTIAN EDUCATION— A POTPOURRI OF KNOWLEDGE

And that from infancy you have known [the] sacred scriptures, which are capable of giving you wisdom for salvation through faith in Christ Jesus. All scripture is inspired by God and is useful for teaching, for refutation, for correction, and for training in righteousness, so that one who belongs to God may be competent, equipped for every good work. (2 Timothy 3:15–17 NARE)

A series of varied definitions have been advanced by various writers, but the critical angle worthy of attention here is to avoid subjecting a complex topic of this nature to a simplistic lineal or straight forward form of definition. For this purpose, I intend to restrict my focus on what promotes a shift in position of the learner from his or her original version to a better version while in the faith journey toward Christ-likeness. This will certainly involve socialization, religious instruction, personal development, and liberation of the mind of the student. Every participant in the process may at one point or the other reconstruct its channel to fit specific needs peculiar to its circumstance for clarity but not deviating from the general features of Christian educational goals. As the society continues to evolve in multicultural composition, we are made aware that various presumptions and new approaches impact participants and the content, as well as the context. Despite the ever-changing demography, the intended shift in the persona of the target group would coalesce into one body in Christ. Christian education is education that caters to the whole person involving cognitive and personality in a fusion with a transactional relationship, bearing in mind that the socialization principle is effective for physical growth and spiritual maturity.

Being a theological discipline as well, Christian education demands that we understand how growth takes place, recognizing that nurturing is a process in which the education being provided is God-centered. The principles adopted constitute simply a compass/GPS for guiding Christian education, and they are incidentally often derived from social sciences but firmly rooted in Scripture. The union of pragmatic theology with the social sciences constitutes the bedrock of Christian education, and so the level of integration paradigm dictates the distinctiveness of Christian education in any educational endeavor and provides the suitable flavor. Christian education is meant to reflect the Christian worldview and must champion character formation and piety in the process. Given that all truth is God's truth, this multifaceted approach is rich enough to serve the present and future evolving complex society and its dynamism. The fulcrum of Christian education is the commitment to the authority of the Bible and to develop Christ-likeness in those being educated. If indeed our faith leads us to love and worship God, it is obvious that we will appreciate the call for transformation and our resolve to embrace discipleship. Practice of Christ-likeness should actually be perceived as aspiration to the Christian way of life. Christian education, to this end, emphasizes the amalgam of perception, theory, and practice in order to synchronize with testimonials always given to graduates, attesting to his/her being *worthy in character and learning*. In light of the above, Christian education continually urges teachers to imbibe the need to work with the divine Teacher as they cannot bring about results in their own power regardless of the depth of their knowledge or skills. Those who are involved or who participate in this transformation, such as parents, church, and school, require the constant invocation of the Holy Spirit to shower the grace of our Lord for their efforts at making disciples as commissioned. Pope Paul VI, in his Declaration on Christian Education, pronounced as follows:

> A Christian education does not merely strive for the maturing of a human person just now described, but has as its principal purpose this goal: That the baptized, while they are gradually introduced to the knowledge of the mystery of salvation, become more aware of the gift of faith

they have received, and that they learn in addition how to worship God the father in spirit and truth (cf. John 4:23) especially in liturgical action, and be conformed in their personal lives according to the new man created in justice and holiness of truth (cf. Eph. 4:22–24) also that they develop into perfect manhood, to the mature measure of the fullness of Christ (cf. Eph. 4:13) and strive for the growth of the physical Body; moreover, that aware of their calling, they learn not only how to bear witness to the hope that is in them (cf. Peter 3:15) but also to help in the Christian formation of the world that takes place when natural powers viewed in the full consideration of man redeemed by Christ contribute to the good of the whole society.[2]

Overall, Christian education is a journey to attain the understanding that faith formation needs in order to be perceived and practiced as a way of life; hence, Christian education is a potpourri of knowledge brewing in church community, stewardship, worship, service, and so forth, being harnessed for the purpose of evangelization with leadership engaged at all levels. Navigating successfully through these windows of opportunity presupposes the existence of sound leadership, which in itself is a clear demonstration of someone with teaching capability. Teaching thus stands in between the present and the future generation with regard to passing on the basic values of life and moral conduct. Consequently, parents and numerous organizations, who want to ensure continuity, are increasingly seeking a genuine form of education where qualified teachers can be found. In the same vein, there is a brimming challenge in developing a leadership cadre for future generations, and this calls for efforts centered on provision of the right caliber of Christian teachers for the needed solution. It is my view herein that Christian education remains the hope for making this provision, given that it draws its authority from the Bible. The following Table 1 provides the biblical foundations of Christian education as the point of reference and affirmation of source of knowledge, content, and principles, as well as context.

Table 1

Biblical Foundations for Christian Education

Passage	Lesson	Target	Duty/Obligation
Matt. 28:19–20	Discipling	Disciples/All believers	Preach unceasingly without fear
Deut. 6:1–9; 2 Tim. 2:24–25; 1Peter 4:10–11	Education	Family/All believers	Educate formally and informally
Deut. 31:9–13	Knowledge of God's laws	All believers	Share knowledge of God and obedience
Ps. 78	Inalienable right of every generation	Intergenerational	Sharing must be passed onto succeeding generation
1 Cor. 12:28–29; 14:26; Eph. 4:7–13	Growth of the church and individual members	All believers	Build up the church and community

Teaching in Christian Education

Before we delve into the subject of understanding teaching in Christian education, it is important to recall the generic concept of a teacher who is perceived as someone who stands in front of a classroom in a choreographed academic setting and tries to enforce the gobbling up of knowledge or facts. The goal is often to get the learner to achieve a predetermined body of knowledge necessary for a specified purpose. Teaching in Christian education transcends this conceptualization. It has its focus on life and draws from the perfect model—Jesus Christ. The goal is transformation of the fallen man back to the image and likeness of God as stated in Genesis, the very first book of the Bible. This was not a mistake. Thus, Christian education deals with the following:

* The focus is on life with the goal of transformation;
* It is scheduled along the life of the target and not one single event— hence, it is a process;
* The training from birth to death requires a teacher at birth, infancy, childhood, early adult, adult, later adult, parents, school, and church as community whereby all get involved;
* Modeling and relationships are critical concerns, emphasizing personality which reflects truths the Scripture communicates in words;
* Making disciples is at the forefront of every action or utterance;
* Mentoring with the gift (charism) of teaching ability is from God for personal edification and of the body of Christ (the church);

* A learning specialist knows the student and the curriculum;
* Teacher and learner share life's experiences together;
* A servant leader is especially equipped by God to take the lead in bringing others to Christ-likeness, and may not necessarily be a classroom expert;
* The teacher-leader guides in a personal love relationship with the Lord by meeting individual needs as the Lord's earthly representative.

In this same line of reasoning, we can then look at the outline of leading or leadership.

Leadership in Christian Education

The generic meaning of leadership simply portrays it as leading a group of people or someone who manages a group of people. Often leadership is interchanged with managing people, especially in the corporate world where leadership is defined by what the objectives of the group or organization are programmed to achieve. Leadership sometimes appears not to have any standard definition other than that it is based on the common denominator—people—the act of leading people. Without bothering on the semantics, one may be tempted to ask if in a journey of two people, one of them would qualify to bear the title of leader. Is leadership synonymous with spokesman? If leading people pluralizes the act of being a leader, then there can be no leader in a party of two. This throws us back to the issue of how best to define leadership. To avoid the chaos of definition and for our perspective in Christian education, leadership assumes dealing with more than two people, given the varied descriptions of the duties of a leader, the stem/root of the word *leadership*.

In his book, *The Art of Leadership*, Max DePree, rather than answer directly to his own question, what is leadership, he responded with: "The first responsibility of a leader is to define reality."[3] Indeed, this is addressing the function of a leader rather than defining leadership or what a leader is. In another breath, he made an outstanding notation about special and eminent leaders who he praised for immense contribution to the growth and success of a specific organization, stating: "In every case, these people have been outstanding teachers."[4] This position thus further suggests that the function of a leader, coach, or guide will determine the success or otherwise in attaining the set goal(s). The approach to reaching an envisaged goal becomes dependent on the qualities of the leadership, which will include but not be limited to vision/creativity, communication, ethics, trust/honesty, knowledge, delegation ability, passion, and so forth. These attributes constitute *elements* of leadership generally and form the basis for evaluation of leadership. De Pree further stated in his *postscript:* "Leadership is much more an art, a belief, a condition of the heart, than a set of things to do. The visible signs of artful leadership are expressed, ultimately, in its practice."[5] He equally indicated what characteristics the organization he was referring to expected of leaders as follows: "from the people chosen to be candidates for future leaders, these must be brought to their responsibilities as they constitute traits that should be present in all leaders:

* has consistent and dependable integrity
* cherishes heterogeneity and diversity
* searches out for competence
* is open to contrary opinion
* communicates easily at all levels
* understands the concept of equity and consistently advocates it
* leads through serving
* is vulnerable to the skills and the talents of others
* is intimate with the organization and its work
* is able to see the broad picture (beyond the area of focus)
* is a spokesperson and diplomat
* can be a tribal storyteller
* tells why rather than how."[6]

Any observer can easily see that these traits deal more with ability to ensure production of goods or services. They are geared toward human material needs with no link or concern for character development.

Leadership in Christian education goes much further than the above secular concept, drawing key elements directly from Scriptures and focusing on life of the "whole person"—spiritually and physically. The elements as provided include:

* Irreproachable (1 Tim. 3: 2).
* Married only once (1 Tim.: 2).
* Must have self-control (1 Tim.3:2).
* Decent (1 Tim. 3:2).
* Hospitable (1 Tim.3:2).

* Not a recent convert (1 Tim. 3:6).
* Must be able to teach (1 Tim. 3:2).
* A servant leader (Matt. 20: 25-28).
* Leadership is not born with/made but summoned by God. Leaders require a special endeavor to get equipped (Eph. 4: 7-14).
* Leaders are considered as elders or overseers or pastor-teachers (Eph.4: 11-13).
* Example setters of Christ-like living (1 Thess.1: 6-7).
* Leadership in the church is seen as multiple in composition in order to offer unity and agreement (Eccles.4: 9-12).

One can easily note from these elements that leading and teaching are virtually inseparable, as the attributes of one are fundamentally similar and interchangeable with the other. There is, however, more to being a teacher than just teaching. The functions of elders are leading or ruling. Teaching is more than talking, although it involves talking at times. In Christian education, leadership assumes the ability to influence someone else while at the same time seeking a better version of oneself in the process. The goal has already been established and provided for us, and we are called upon to emulate as being directed by the wisdom we acquire as we grow through the power of the Holy Spirit. Our Lord and Savior Jesus Christ has set the standard and with faith and the grace of God, whoever is called simply falls in line. Leadership in Christian education does not lend itself to open-ended definitions and cannot therefore be designed to meet some new goals.

Leadership is defined with clarity in Christian education to avoid contradictions, unlike in the secular arena like in, say, network marketing wherein Dr. Tom Barret in his book, *Dare to Dream and Work*, says "leadership can be defined in numerous ways." And as an example he states: "leadership is showing someone the way and then stepping out of the way."[7] This definition clearly contradicts the very essence of the student becoming his teacher and a coheir as taught in Christian education. Here the spirit of replication for getting disciples is ripped apart, given that spiritual maturity is a process and as such requires time and practice with necessary reinforcement. In the light of this reasoning, we can discern that leadership definitions that abound are shaped by specific needs of organizations and bound by time. Whenever the needs of the organization change, the structure and frame of reference for leadership training is automatically altered to reflect the new ideology. That explains the reason why some organizations stress the need to leave a legacy after serving as a leader, some talk of nurturing the roots of the institution, and others say a leader is one who knows the way and is able to encourage others to tag along. There is yet another that says: "Leadership is a concept of owing certain things to the institution. It is a way of thinking about institutional heirs, a way of thinking about stewardship as contrasted with ownership."

These varied "definitions," which are actually descriptions of functions, may fit exceedingly well in achieving corporate objectives in a products or services environment but are certainly anemic in the context of Christian education. The concepts of leadership and teaching are both sourced from

Scriptures as shown in Tables 2 and 3 below. They serve as foundations for teaching and leadership in Christian education in view of Peter's exhortation: "Each one should use whatever spiritual gift he has received to serve others, faithfully administering God's grace in its various forms. If anyone speaks, he should do it as one speaking the very words of God. If anyone serves, he should do it with the strength God provides, so that in all things God may be praised through Jesus Christ. To Him be the glory and the power for ever and ever. Amen" (1 Pet. 4:10–11).

Undoubtedly, Christian education is *not* a made-up idea of some overzealous members of the Christian community or some noisy group searching for a niche in the educational arena to pitch their tent of specialization. It is *not* a mere theoretical construct, either. The topic of leadership and teaching which form the basis of these arguments are theologically situated in line with biblical application. As earlier posited herein, knowledge content in Christian education is drawn from the Bible and the following Tables 2 and 3 refer to the biblical foundations.

Table 2
Biblical Foundations for Teaching

Passage	Lesson	Target/ Group	Duty/Obligation
Rom. 8:1–27; Gal. 5:16–26; Acts 1:1 John 14:26; 1 Cor. 2:13	Guide	Entire faithful	Seek the help of the Holy Spirit
Matt. 28:20; Acts 14:21; Mark 6:30; Luke12:12; Acts 18:24–28	Learn how to teach	Apostles	Acquire knowledge
Rom. 12:3–8; 1 Cor.12:27–31; Eph. 4:7–13; 29; 5:15–22; 1 Pet. 4:10–11	Gift from God	Church	Deploy it for edification of self and the people; Show commitment.
Exod. 35:34; Isa. 29:11;12; Jer.1:6;6:15; Matt. 2:1	Ability/ integrity; competence	All faithful	Be approachable
Matt. 2;1; 1 Cor. 2:13–16;	Wisdom	All faithful	Be intimate while vulnerable to their charism, sharing with others
Luke 24:13–35	Listening/ attentive	Disciples	Pay attention with what happens around you
1 Tim. 5:17	Respect/honor	Disciples	Be committed & consistent
2 Tim. 2:2	Evangelization/ discipling	All faithful	Never stop teaching

Table 3
Biblical Foundations for Leadership

Passage	Lesson	Target Group	Duty/Obligation
1 Tim. 5:17; Titus 1:6–7; John 13:14'	Leading/ ruling	Disciples	Be dutiful and exemplary
Acts 20:28–30;1 Pet. 5:2	Shepherding/ discipling	Disciples	Be vigilant
Eph. 4:11–13; 1 Tim. 3:1–2; 1 Pet. 4:10–11; Matt. 28;19–20; John 15:27	Teaching/ education	Disciples	Use your gifts for building up; testify
Titus 1:8–9	Discipline	Disciples	Be knowledgeable and consistent
1 Tim. 3:1–7; 3:8–12; 1 Pet. 5:3–4; Matt. 20:25–26	Rendering of service	All believers	Be trustworthy and exude confidence and humility
Heb. 5:11–14	Relationships	Disciples	Do not be tired of learning
1 Thess. 1:6–7	Modeling	Disciples	Imitate the Lord and the apostles

There are also specific biblical directives for leaders that are useful to feature here, such as the following:

> Holding fast to the true message as taught so that he will be able to exhort with sound doctrine and to refute opponents (Titus 1:9).

You know that the rulers of the gentiles… them; But it shall not be so among you. Rather, whoever wishes to be great among you shall be your servant (Matt. 20:25–26).

And you became imitators of us and of the lord, receiving the word in great affliction, with joy from the Holy Spirit, so that you became a model for all the believers (1Thess. 1:6–7).

Go make disciples of all nations…Holy Spirit; teaching them to observe all that I have commanded you (Matt. 28:19–20).

And you also testify, because you have been with me from the beginning (John 15:27).

Tend the flock of God in your midst (overseeing) not by constraint but willingly, as God would have it, not for shameful profit but eagerly. Do not lord it over those assigned to you, but be examples to the flock (1 Pet. 5:2–3).

From the perspective of specificity, certain words in the quotes above present some prominence inherent in the instructions and will continue to be featured in this leadership and teaching discourse. These include: Teach, imitate, servant, model, make disciples, tend, testify, and sometimes their derivatives as the case may be. Each word is explained and clearly defined in one part of the scripture or another to ensure there is no misinterpretation or undue representation in line of truth. Man's follow-up actions have tended to distort this focus in the secular world.

CHAPTER 2

PERCEPTION OF TEACHING IN THE SECULAR WORLD

Teaching tends to present differing images to various professional callings. In the Preface to his book, *The Art of Teaching*, Jay Parini, states: "Teaching is not only a job of work. A teacher is charged with waking students to the nature of reality, providing rigorous introduction to a certain discipline, and creating an awareness of their responsibility as citizens trained in the art of critical thinking." For him, this is the perception of the proprietor of a school or whoever engages the services of a teacher. Later in the book, he comes up with what he describes as the perception teachers have of themselves: "Teachers often seem to believe they are invisible in the classroom, but this is impossible, a fantasy. Teaching is after all, a performance art where we assume a costume of sorts every day of the semester. We send countless messages, explicit and implicit, to our students, who are reading us as closely as they read their texts. Evidently, they are bound to copy us from whatever color."[8]

These views from both an observer and a doer fall in tandem with the recurring words of Scripture, associated with teaching as mentioned above. In addition, the place of teaching in human development features such clear prominence that makes it difficult to ignore its presence in building a whole life. Teaching was considered so crucial that the Holy Spirit placed it as one of the foundational gifts to the church; hence teachers enjoy automatic community respect. Additionally, there is even a warning about a more severe judgment reserved for those holding the office or duty. The teacher is, therefore, endowed with the ability to help people to learn from the standpoint that they assist others to grow in Christ-likeness. The teacher manipulates the human outer factors with the inner ones to influence positive change in behavior with the help of the Holy Spirit. He guides changes by helping to meet the learners' immediate needs, thereby preparing them for future encounters based on present experience and helping them to assume responsibilities in their own affairs with the understanding that all fall under God's authority.

"Go make disciples of all nations." We cannot carry out this commission without being a teacher, I believe. Given that it is directed to all believers and has no time limit, the church relies on those who have been prepared to champion the course. In our present dispensation, available statistics show a remarkable decline in the number of aspirants to priesthood, pastors, Christian teachers, and different categories of ordained people of God. These devoted humans do not drop from the sky but are rather members of families where they are first exposed to strong roots in church activities, usually taking root from parental involvement in church matters, which creates a foundation for their children's interest in pastoral life and may then lead, for some, to formation as Christian teachers or even the priesthood. Within this context, we may also fit in stewardship, which is now erroneously interpreted to mean money matters only, totally excluding the upbringing of children entrusted to us.

Occasionally, one can determine the kind of background of a growing child by his spontaneous response to a situation. For purpose of illustration, there is this short folklore story told as follows: A little three- or four-year-old boy went to a corner shop with his father to buy some groceries. On their way out, the shop owner graciously offered the boy some mixed nuts, which were conspicuously displayed in a red bowl by the exit door. He said to the boy whose father was immediately behind him: "Dip your hand and scoop some nuts for yourself, son." Instead of quickly reaching for it, the boy turned and looked up to his dad. The store owner repeated himself, imagining that the boy was not sure of the offer. "Go ahead, son, and get yourself a handful of nuts. It's free." The boy repeated his earlier gesture, turned and looked up to his father without uttering a word and not doing a thing, either. His father then stretched his own hand and scooped out a handful of nuts and filled the boy's open hand and retained what was left for a refill. The little boy turned to the store owner and shouted out loud, "Thank you, sir" and left the store with his dad.

Several interpretations or conclusions can be drawn from this simple illustration, but what I consider outstanding is the positivity and character of the parents manifested here that cannot be separated from this boy's admirable conduct. The family, which constitutes the first church unit, generates the foundation for character formation and is the first teaching and learning platform. Teaching, therefore, begins at home, and the "professional teacher" continues with the process. The teacher stands in position to imitate and practice the life of Christ by maturing equally in the privilege and responsibilities of life in Christ, which enable him to work creatively to "apprehend that for which we were apprehended of Christ." Pastors and teachers fall into a single group in the Greek language, shepherding congregations. Teachers are also trainers in Christian education because they are concerned with transformation of the Christian into a Christ-like citizen of the church. Herein the teacher must be a person living in faith while reflecting the meaning of biblical truths. So being a Christian teacher in the church is multidimensional since it goes beyond mere lecturing. Jesus's invitation to Simon Peter to "Follow me and I will make you fishers of men" in effect is: I will make you like Me, which parallels "Whatever you have learned or received or heard from me, or seen in me– put into practice. And the God of peace will be with you" (Phil.4:9). Each parallel to this instruction in scripture essentially projects leaders to be viewed as teachers in order to provide models and develop a family relationship within which the modeling process can easily take place. The teacher is here to guide, show examples, instruct, influence, groom, and make disciples. Richards puts it this way: "We must recognize the teacher as a leader especially equipped by God to take the lead in bringing others to Christ's likeness—not as the classroom expert."[9]

Leadership

From a similar point of specificity as given directly in the Scriptures, we can note certain key words acting as prominent directives for qualities and expectations of leadership; we find—be a servant, imitators in order to model, make disciples, teach, testify, tend (oversee), be an example, be reputable, be filled with the Spirit and wisdom, and so forth. These words all capture the fact that leadership also is a process of influencing someone and parallels the duty to be exemplary. One can easily feel and perceive that the primary concern in recognizing men as leaders is brought about by character and exemplary behavior. And within the church, leadership assumes multiple or plurality in form rather than singularity for decision-making. Given the need for maturity in Christ, leadership gets restricted to those who have been groomed while recent converts are explicitly excluded.

Knowledge

The leader is seen as the reservoir of knowledge in whatever activity he or she is engaged. As also in the secular world where he may not be an expert in any known field, he should know where to obtain information or material necessary with which to carry out the needed activity. He is seen to be nearer to the necessary resources to ensure that the group/organization remains a going concern and not in doubt at any point in time. Knowledge has a much wider meaning in the Bible and goes beyond understanding, recognition, and an acknowledgment in definition. It incorporates the idea of a deeper appreciation of something or a relationship with someone. It should be noted that knowledge of God remains the most valuable knowledge for a human being to possess but is not sufficient without an in-depth appreciation for and a relationship with Him. As Christians, our constant resort to Christ "in whom are hidden all the treasures of wisdom and knowledge" (Col. 2:2–3) is because knowledge implies a relationship. Increasing in the knowledge of God is part of Christian maturity and something all Christians are expected to experience as we "grow in the knowledge of our Lord and savior Jesus Christ" (2 Pet. 3:18). So knowledge is what is acquired over time. It is always expected that knowledge goes hand-in-hand with wisdom because if anyone lacks knowledge, he will lack wisdom. The Bible nonetheless reminds us that human knowledge apart from God is flawed; hence, the pursuit of knowledge for its own sake, without seeking God, is foolishness. Leaders are therefore cautioned to lead with honesty and truth in line with Christ— the truth as He told His disciples, "You will know the truth and the truth shall set you free" (John 8:32).

Vision/Creativity

This deals with the ability to articulate the trajectory of the community and motivate the people toward achieving the goal being, in this case, the purpose for which God created man. It will involve coaching, modeling, and feedback for the individual as well as corporate growth. The teacher/

leader promotes and guides opportunities for people to exploit their creativity as part of corporate energy and assets. In any sudden turn of events the leader is looked upon to create or figure out a way forward. It is important to mention here the fact that some radical religious educators argue that Divine authority impedes creativity, whereas it actually offers broad room for creativity. After all, creation or the word *create* came to prominence from Scripture and can be traced back to Genesis and, of course, is validated by the varied gifts of the Holy Spirit made available to man for human capacity to be creative.

Purpose

The biblical sense of purpose connotes the encompassing coverage of God's intention for an individual's life along with those around him/her through the process of growth—from home to school, work, community, and society at large. There is, thus, a purpose for everyone. No one was born without a purpose, and it is affirmed in Christianity that every one of our plans should be anchored on God's plan since the latter is the only one that lasts. In this regard, we are always encouraged to be patient, hence the good old prayer - thy will be done. We are also conscious of the fact that God programmed everything for our own good even when our human thought may not quite understand it at difficult times. After all, situations that we deem rough and tough may turn out with something positive. A sad experience may turn out to be a blessing in disguise. We do remember and appreciate the horrific event—that happened on a certain Friday which today bears the name Good Friday! Overall, therefore, our vision or creativity as articulated earlier, as the case may be, are subsumed in God's purpose for us as human beings, and whatever aspirations we may have should be tamed to align with it. Several references exist as evidence but for our discourse two will suffice herein:

> Many are the plans in a person's heart, but it is
> the Lord's purpose that prevails (Prov. 19:21).

Therefore, my dear friends as you have always obeyed—not only in my presence, but, now much more in my absence—continue to work out your salvation with fear and trembling, for it is God who works in you to will and to act in order to fulfill his good purpose (Phil. 2:12– 13).

We must remember at all times that God and His purposes are perfect, but we are not.

Communication

This comes along the fact that a leader is seen as a teacher, and the prerequisite for teaching and learning is ability to communicate effectively. In every organization, there are issues that tend to form a seeming gridlock requiring technical knowledge to unlock. Communication acts as the key for untying any such knot and is obviously one empowering element leaders have but often gets relegated to the background while seeking for a solution to a variety of human activities, especially issues connected with leadership. Subordinates tend to evaluate their leaders by the manner a leader communicates. Humane approach naturally hits human reaction such that a subordinate who feels being reckoned with will most likely realize and appreciate that they are all working together toward a common goal as opposed to feeling that she/he is working for—them. The informal communication, which often echoes in the phrase "action speaks louder than words" is the pivot of this illustrated sentiment. The Christian education principle of socialization propounds the strong impact it has on modeling for making disciples. It also has bearing on formal and informal ways of educating. Followers have been shown to be more interested in working with a leader who manifests character by portraying the ability to speak and act with conviction, and cognizance of the humanity of those being spoken to or with, as the case may be; who endeavors to also listen to the subordinate(s), build trust, and not failing to compliment when appropriate, creating a strong sense of belonging and offering support to enable acceptance of change. It is through their communication method/style that leaders steer the group/organization in the proper direction. A visible level of certainty to show that the leader is working toward building up, that is, empowering his/her subordinate can easily result in the claiming and feeling of collective ownership in the effort. Communication within the community provides the bonding wire that keeps the system in motion. The leader is the engine of the control room through his communication skills, whereby he constantly gives clarification to all ambiguities. In our present-day context, he has a variety of media at his disposal, such as email, fax, telephone, texting, FaceTime, Twitter, Facebook, and Instagram as channels for this purpose.

Trust/Honesty

Honesty is truthfulness. To be honest is to be truthful or sincere. The truthfulness of our words is often proved by the honesty of our conduct. No one can be consistently honest without a commitment to the truth, but the leader is advised to be conscious of the fact that at times, being honest can hurt someone's feelings. It does not mean then that dishonesty be preferred in the circumstance. The Christian education point of view here is that honesty means speaking the truth which is an acceptable quality in human interaction. Evading truth in order to avoid conflict can be very costly at the end. Since we focus and uphold in Christian education God's purpose in our leadership and teaching, honesty and truth play a vital role in the way we conduct our daily activities. We hold dear the idea of reflecting the character of God who we know is truthful and loving. Being a leader in any community grants one the opportunity to show the light for others to follow while realizing that it can sometimes be discomforting to speak the truth. Above all, as children of God (John 1:12), in whom there is no dishonesty, our lives should be swaddled in His truth, and we should be honest in all we say and do.

Honesty is motivated by love and not as a result of some form of obsession with providing what may be perceived to be accurate information at a point in time. Members within the group/organization and along its various hierarchy of trust believe that every statement emanating from the leader is honest and worthy of being followed to both the letter and spirit because any deficiency can be catastrophic for the future of such group/organization. Trust is naturally the foundation to human relationship. Notwithstanding that man may at some point breach the trust reposed in him, it does not call for a decision never to trust again, knowing that the one who breached the trust cannot be expected to do what only God is and does. But we know that when we live by trusting each other, we edify ourselves individually and corporately as a group. Christian leadership is known to be a role that must not only be played but in reality lived. The heart of Christian leadership is honesty and integrity, demonstrated through genuine commitment to the goals and values of the group being led. The members of the group must also recognize that quality in their leader and strive to be truthful with one another, even when such honesty becomes painful or produces discomfort in feeling.

Ethics

Ethics is applied by Christian leaders as a guide to promoting morality in courses of action as well as the goodness of individuals and groups toward living a good life. It concerns other people's interest, and snowballing into societal interest, with regard to the way they make decisions and lead their lives in pursuit of God's purpose. The principles they garner from Scriptures help them to determine the ethical course of any given situation. The leader provides the flags of moral and ethical conduct within the community, and all other members borrow from him/her what is acceptable as appropriate behavior. This does not conflict with the fact that individuals in the group may have the basic common sense of what is right and wrong. In addition, the leader is the image maker of the group outside the physical location and so is expected to be sensitive to the values and ideals of the context in which they operate. It is important to state here that in Christian education, it will be incomplete to talk about ethics without mentioning God. I believe that since questions of nature can be clarified by religion as provided in the Bible rather than questions of religion being clarified by nature, relationship is always emphasized as well as recommended because it offers a broader template for community growth and spiritual maturity toward man's salvation. This may not necessarily be seen to be so in the secular world.

CHAPTER 3

PRACTICAL APPLICATION OF LEADERSHIP/CRISIS IN DEFINITION

In defining leadership or a leader as is the convention in the secular world, each writer carefully and wittingly introduces a caveat or some form of modifier such as a successful leader, an effective leader, or a good leader, and so on. Leadership in the corporate world is dressed in different colorations in order to establish their primacy in the organization to ensure their fruitful performance. They are equally exposed to situations where wisdom is seen or can be seen to have been applied. In an answer to the question "Are managers leaders?" an author, Abraham Zaleznik, responded:

> In considering the development of leadership, we have two different courses of life history: (1) development through socialization which prepares the individual to guide institutions and to maintain the existing balance of social

relation; and (2) development through mastery, which impels an individual to struggle for psychological and social change. Society produces its managerial talents through the first line of development; leaders emerge through the second.[10]

This falls in tandem with a Christian approach to leadership, which is predicated on process, continuity, and the future, all standing on the framework of change. His position here right away ascribes this important training through socialization to managers rather than to leaders. He goes further to explore the interlocking relationship of teaching and leadership by stating:

> The only sure way an individual can interrupt reverie-like preoccupation and self-absorption is to form a deep attachment to a great teacher or other person who understands and has the ability to communicate with the gifted individual. Whether gifted individuals find what they need in one-to-one relationships depends on the availability of teachers, possibly parental surrogates whose strengths lie in cultivating talent."[11]

He goes on to advocate "Fortunately, when generations meet and the self-selections occur, we learn more about how to develop leaders and how talented people of different generations influence each other. Great teachers take risks. They bet initially on talent they perceive on younger people.

The risks do not always pay off, but the willingness to take them appears to be crucial in developing leaders.[12]

As an example of the risk teachers take, it becomes interesting to hear from a group of teachers whose goal was to change a long-standing notion in America that pupils living in low-income neighborhoods do not and cannot achieve well and as high in academics compared to their counterparts who are in high-income neighborhoods. They developed what they called leadership principles where they propounded six rubrics, guiding how their teachers work with set strategies for effective delivery of teaching in order to close the achievement gap of children within low-income areas in North America. The notion in the locality is that children caught in the socioeconomic inequities are inhibited by schools within low-income communities from making impact on their academic achievement. The tendency has been to hold onto the belief that it is not efficacious to invest in mitigating the challenges of poverty that makes it hard for students to focus on school. The consequence is said to be a cycle of low academic achievement that has created an achievement gap between children brought up in low-income communities as compared to their counterparts in high-income communities. The work by the organization has disproved the belief through "teaching as leadership," and having succeeded by making a difference in the performance of children in low-income communities, it has now become the title of a book by Steven Farr. Rather than adorn themselves as teachers, they went for strategies that make them function as "LEADERS at every level of educational system, at every level of policy, and across all professional sectors believe deeply that educational inequity is a solvable problem." This also embodies the belief that "they are in control of and ultimately responsible for their students' success or failure." And, with hard work, the leaders (teachers) and their students can make dramatic progress in spite of whatever burden poverty places on pupils from low-income communities. The rubrics, or leadership principles, whereby teaching is perceived as leadership in their approach reflect the following:

1. Set big goals that are ambitious, measurable, and meaningful for their students;
2. Invest students and their families through a variety of strategies to reach those ambitious goals;
3. Plan purposefully—focus on where students are headed, using the most efficient path;
4. Execute effectively—monitor progress and adjust where necessary;
5. Continuously increase effectiveness—identify root causes and find solutions; and
6. Work relentlessly—give their conviction that they have the power to work past obstacles for student leaders.

My sincere reaction is that these once more are characteristics of leadership shrouded in teaching methods. In the Foreword to the book, *Teaching as Leadership*, Jason Kamras, National Teacher of the Year 2005, stated: "Excellent teachers can make a dramatic difference in children's lives. In fact, I believe that teachers are the locus of power in the fight to close the achievement Gap." In this regard, therefore, the label for teachers and leaders is shown to be interchangeable. Jason went further to say that the teachers who are successful at closing the achievement gap "do exactly what great leaders do when they face seemingly insurmountable odds." As shown here, the teaching capability has functioned as a lifting rod for underprivileged pupils out of low academic achievement.

Modern Management and Leadership

Leadership today can be seen to have over the years metamorphosed to a mere "person in front" or "my up-line" and is particularly tied to an organization. To this extent, whatever elements are associated with the term must conform to the goals, which are often the bottom line of the respective organization. The church unwittingly has succumbed to this new definition and is constantly adopting "modern management" theories to supplant leadership as conceived within the church circle. Church lay members often get frustrated when the clergy resist practicing the modern professional management standards. It should not be difficult to understand that given their vocational training, the expected role appears seriously at variance with the traditional understanding of leadership and especially now that theological language has yielded to secular terms and nuances. When the church refers to whole-person approach, it is understood to mean the physical and the spiritual, while the secular world understands it as the involvement of those higher up, meaning those the leader is responsible to, those down, the subordinates; and those across, the peers and associates outside the hierarchy.

Leadership and Ownership Structure

Amidst the pressure brought about by the superfluous changes in concepts is the huge privatization of the church, which in itself promotes business practices and principles. In order to run these privately owned churches which are often inundated with jobs pegged not only with job descriptions but also with contracts of employment, they invoke the anger of the vocation-oriented members. Thus, variation in human activities has cropped leadership to fit into a new understanding of the elements of leadership in contrast to what is professed in Christian education.

Leadership and Individual Aspirations

As it stands, leadership in the modern secular world is clearly under siege. Everyone seems to now stay safe in defining what leadership is but would rather describe the qualities an effective leader should have and those are made to stumble through for the "elements" of leadership to give coverage to its relative definition. In some jurisdictions, they are labeled *traits* while in others they are simply *principles* of either a leader or leadership. These labels often, if not always, include integrity, initiative, innovation, insight, interest, information, inspiration, and so forth. Nonetheless, educators are very aware of this crisis in the conceptual frame of reference in leadership. In his book, *Called to Lead*, John F. MacArthur states clearly:

> Both Church and world seem to have traded
> away the notion of leadership for celebrity.
> Today's heroes are people who are famous for

being famous. They are not necessarily (and not even usually) men and women of character. Real leadership is in seriously short supply." He did not stop at that but goes further to remind us that the world is crying out "… for leaders-great heroic, noble trust worthy leaders. We need leaders at every level of the social order-from political leaders in the international realm to spiritual leaders in the church and the family. And most people recognize that need.[13]

It is also important to note here that he is referring mainly to the issue in leadership, which is often not included in the common list of qualities such as earlier given herein. He then concludes thus: "The problem is that we live in an era where the very definition of character has become fussy. People bemoan the loss of integrity in general terms, but few have any clear idea of what 'integrity' entails anymore. Moral standards have been systematically obliterated. Virtually no clear moral or ethical standards are universally accepted anymore."

Leadership and Personal Convictions

In the midst of this seemingly confused atmosphere shrouding the definition of leadership and its derivatives, another author, Albert R. Mohler in his book, *The Conviction to Lead*, comes up with what he thinks should bring a change in the foundations of leadership. He stated right at the beginning of the book: "Let me warn you right up front— my goal is to change the way you think about leadership.

I do not aim to add one more voice to the conversation about leadership, I want fundamentally to change the way leadership is understood and practiced." He then went on to submit two relevant issues of interest from the Christian perspective that tie with his worldview of leadership. He argues first it is imperative for a leader to have a worldview-casting ability for leading and guiding the organization or group, and secondly that a leader must be passionate about the core beliefs and mission of the organization he leads. Using his own experiences and knowledge from history, he practically demonstrated that "real leadership is transferring convictions to others, affecting their actions, motivations, intuitions, and commitment."[14] One can easily see he is looking at a fundamental change of the mind and nature of the leader without falling into the trap of offering a list of leadership qualities and the way to do things.

New Directions in Leadership

As if this kind of alteration is the new direction, another well-known author, Philip Selznick, in his book, *Leadership in Administration*, propounds: "Leadership is not a familiar, everyday idea, as readily available to common sense as to social sciences. It is a slippery phenomenon that eludes both." By so claiming it eludes both common sense and social sciences, he has introduced a new concept, thus removing the meaning out of everyday conversational matter. He then comes up with what he says should define leadership, which he insists should include: (1) a kind of work done to meet social needs; (2) not equivalent to office-holding or high prestige or decision-making; and

(3) dispensable (theoretically, for an institution). He then espouses: "An institutional leader … is primarily an expert in the promotion of values."[15]

We are here thrown right back to the field of "definition through description" but with an addendum that leadership is dispensable. Selznick's argument quickly turns its focus to the word *coach* that appears to be rather specific and on target from the perspective of everyday use and common understanding. From a practical bearing, it will be useful at this point to consider what a sports professional, a coach, has to say about leadership. In his book, *Above the Line*, Urban Meyer, a famous American football coach, gave an insight in the prologue titled "Leading from the Heart," into what role a leader plays in winning games. He stresses what he called the foundation playbook, which I grant will sound better when put in his own words:

> "Leadership isn't a difference maker, it is *the* difference maker. Talent will get you about seven or eight wins. Discipline pushes it to nine wins, maybe. But when you add leadership, that's when the magic happens."[16] "… Every day is a battle for how well you will live your life: Above the line or Below the line; Above the line behavior is intentional on purpose and skillful. Below the line behavior is impulsive, on autopilot, and resistant. Getting and staying Above the Line is the foundation for success in anything you do. It does not come naturally. It must be taught and learned…. It starts with leadership. If you want

the people on your team to perform Above the line, then you must live *Above the Line.*[17]

In relation to characteristics/traits of a leader, he recommends:

"Invest the time to think. Make it a priority. Leaders think deeply, originally, and often, bravely. When things aren't going right, the most important thing you can do is slow down, go deep, and figure out why. Encourage your people to bring new ideas to you. And when they do, listen. … Exceptional leaders think about common things in an uncommon way."[18]

Finally he affirms: "The highest levels of performance are empowered by the deepest levels of belief. … Belief creates vision. It sees the invisible. It sees the goal and pathway that are required to accomplish the goal."[19]

Professional Outlook on Leadership

Unlike in the Sports profession, fire-fighting has its own mindset with regards to leadership and professional outlook. The picture is beautifully illustrated in the following piece from Firehouse.org.

From a professional arena, Firehouse, on its website, propounds clearly what they call 8 Essential Elements of Effective leadership. It is equally good to reproduce their position here in their own words to enable the reader have a true feel of their passion:

"Eight elements (qualities) that a real leader possesses:

1. Integrity is the first and most important of the elements of leadership. It is the little voice inside you that tells you when you are not telling the truth or taking an action that you know will unjustly hurt someone;

2. Initiative is the second element of leadership. A real leader will be the one that gets the ball rolling. Nothing happens in any organization, public or private without someone taking the initiative and getting things going;

3. Innovation is a mandatory element of fire service leadership. Each and every situation we face is different;

4. Insight is a quality that may take years to develop. Leaders must have insight into their organization's mission statement, a real understanding of exactly what it is that we are supposed to be doing it for;

5. Interest is what is going on, how it is being done, and who is doing the work is another important hallmark of leadership;

6. Inspiration is hard to put your finger on but when it's there it's hard to hold onto with both hands. Inspiration is a thought or feeling that drives us to action; internal drive that helps or even forces us to get up and get something done;

7. Intensity is a quality that not all leaders have, but one that all great leaders need. Intensity is the level, the speed, the height, the depth, the drive to get the job done and to get it done right, exactly right;

8. Information is an important element of any business but it is vital in the fire rescue service. Information sharing is a continuous process that goes up and down the chain of command and horizontally as well. Leaders must master the art of information sharing and utilize this avenue of communication to better prepare their subordinates for the tasks at hand and those that lie ahead in the future."[20]

From their follow-up discourse, one will easily realize that the basis of their position as given above is that they see "a leadership void" and, as they allege, it is supposedly hurting their operational standard. The reason is because of the focus on making money rather than quality of service. An observer can easily discern that this distortion in goals and objectives impacts heavily on the elements that have been lucidly articulated but does not drill us out of the deep crisis afflicting a generally acceptable definition of leadership.

Leadership and Culture

To avoid escalating the situation, a large number of authors now get around it by seeking some refinement by way of citing cultural changes and technological development. It may sound obvious and convincing to insist on evoking a fresh look at how the term *leadership* is perceived in our present multicultural society. In this direction of forging out a new window of definition, Heifetz posits strongly that we should abandon the idea that "leaders are born and not made." He presents a new theory of leadership with a view to bringing to light two important distinctions he calls technical and adaptive problems in leadership and authority. He is of the view that leadership is more of an activity, rather than a position of influence. He appears to hover his mouse over the "technical" problems besetting a leader and discovers they can be solved by expertise and good management while the "adaptive" problems, such as poverty, racial tensions, and drug abuse require innovation and learning. He then goes further to propound that the task of the leader is to close the gap so created. His belief that leaders are made rather than born is quite in sync with the concept of transformation as well as discipleship in Christian education. This also falls in line with our quest to determine if teaching is an essential element of leadership, which we shall later examine in full. It is proper to note here that if someone is born a leader, he would have no need then to be taught or learn from someone else. Heifetz's submission that adaptive problems can better be solved through innovation and learning resonates with the current movement to legalize the use of certain drugs considered illegal in parts of the Western world. He also interestingly addresses what he calls "leadership without authority" and says "while we usually focus attention at the head of the table, leadership may more often emerge from the foot of the table."[21] He further exemplifies this by stating that leaders without authority "push us to clarify our values, face hard realities, and seize new possibilities however frightening they may be."[22]

Leadership in New Cloaks

The trend thus continues in seeking new windows of leadership definition in order to get off what has sometimes been considered as a path of mundane/ambiguous formulations. This trend has equally brought to the fore the seeming confusion at the doorsteps of organizations being viewed as providers of hierarchical framework for determining and distinguishing managers from leaders. Selznick categorically stated along this line: "The idea is developed in this essay that leadership is not equally necessary in all large-scale organizations, or in any one at all times, and that it becomes dispensable as the natural processes of institutionalization become eliminated or controlled."[23] One can see that this may sound good and appears sensible in today's world of multi-performing technological gadgets and robots, but certainly shows a summersault from what we know in Christian education and espouse as leadership from modeling and influencing coupled with discipleship. The view equally knocks the efforts of those involved in leading major multinational organizations charged with cross-national boundaries as well as differing managerial jurisdictions that require global leadership responsibilities. Here is where leadership cuts across a network of companies beyond one hierarchical entity. The challenges in this situation become more complicated, thereby rendering the decision-making capabilities and control somehow redundant. It is in the light of this that Dr. Leonard Marcus, Dr. Barry Dorn and Joseph Henderson, who have been at the forefront in the leadership framework, came up with the concept of "meta-leadership" that addresses leadership challenges that cross inter- as well as intra-organizational demarcations. This focuses on a unified action of all stakeholders toward a common goal of which leaders are expected to lead *down* in the traditional sense, *up* to influence the people they are accountable to, and *across* to peer groups and others with whom there is no formal subordinate relationship.

This model, developed at Harvard University, puts it as an integrated whole and so the form involving such broad and overarching leadership is what is defined in this new window of definition as meta-leadership. Rather than add to the existing elements of leadership, it tends to create more theoretical concept about leadership in an attempt to modernize the same to fit what is perceived to be today's organization.

Collective Approach to Leadership

Peter Senge, author of a book entitled, *The Fifth Discipline*, floated yet another new proposition, submitting that as the world becomes more interconnected and business becomes more complex and dynamic, work must become more "learningful." He propounds that it is no longer sufficient to have one person learning for an organization. According to him, it is just not possible any longer to figure out solutions from the top, and have everyone else follow the orders of the "grand strategist." He equally thinks the organizations that will truly excel in the future will be those that discover how to tap people's commitment and capability to learn at all levels in the organization. He therefore proposes what he calls a "learning organization," which he says is possible because "deep down we are all learners. No one has to teach an infant to learn. In fact no one has to teach an infant anything. They are intrinsically inquisitive, masterful learners who learn to walk, speak and pretty much run their households all on their own. Learning organizations are possible because not only is it our nature to learn but we love to learn."[24] In its review of the book, *Fortune Magazine* came forcefully on the idea and wrote: "Forget your old, tired ideas about leadership. The most successful corporation of the 1990s will be something called a learning organization."[25] And following in its wake, another, unnamed reviewer added thus: "Learning organizations— corporations that overcome obstacles to learning, and develop dynamic ways to pin point the threats that face them and to recognize new opportunities. Not only is the learning organization a new source of competitive advantage, it also offers a marvelously empowering approach to work, one which promises that as Archimedes puts it, 'with a lever long enough…single-handed, I can move the world.'"[26]

Leadership and technology

As it stands, the confusion and contradictions over leadership continue unabated in several directions without anyone examining what the common elements are in the midst of the ever-changing human and technological dynamics. To my knowledge nobody is making any serious effort to resolve it for the benefit of everyday thought and understanding. However, the argument is bound to continue until there is a pronounced shift in focus from an organization-centered approach I will call "organ-centric" to a human-centered approach, otherwise called "human-centric." It is my view that the church would have to lead this change of focus, being the custodian of truth, and should not painfully continue to adopt and rely on procedures and practices originated in secular organizations and institutions. The church's failure to initiate or champion knowledge creativity has led members to express frustration at what they perceive as failures in good management practice and accountability as they continue to judge from a secular leadership aperture. This has strangely led to a general inability to distinguish between paid employment with an attached job description with a vocation, and volunteer function traditionally practiced along Christian leadership benchmarks. Compounding the situation is the advent of the privatization of religion, bringing forth the uncertainty and clarity as to the role of the laity versus that of the ordained ministers/clergy with regard to leadership. Also in jeopardy is the use of their variety of gifts and time within the turbulent atmosphere. Following this path, I believe, will certainly lead us back to the truth that Christian education fosters and is always expressed in promoting Christian self-understanding but is somehow slow in providing its own appropriate language for elements related to leadership. This position is well articulated by Mervin Davis and Graham Dodds in their Foreword to *Leadership in the Church for People of Hope*, as they stated: "We believe that while it is right to insist on good institutional practice, the church and its ministry are not simply to be understood in management terms. The solution to some of the difficulties that have been experienced in the past are not likely to be solved simply by the imposition of secular models of contemporary organizational practice." And while this approach may seem awkward to multinationals and profit-oriented organizations, it is equally the view of some influential advocates. London Business School, for example, on their website, starts a conversation on the above subject with the following bold advert:

Act, speak and think like a leader? If not what's in your way?— successful leadership is about acting and thinking like a leader, activating your best self and unlocking potentials in others. So to define purpose, build credibility and exercise influence, start by asking hard questions about who you are and what you stand for. As a senior executive you need to set the direction and influence others—at times without authority. How can you do that, if your perceived "fatal flaws" are getting in the way of you achieving your best as a leader?

This encapsulates clearly the idea and need for racing back to the Christian education human-centered approach in training leaders. Being obstinate about rethinking leadership to arrive at a unity of purpose and in line with biblical truth may certainly not be a useful escape route for societal advancement.

CHAPTER 4

BIBLICAL FOUNDATION OF TEACHING

From the Old Testament, we learn about teaching as "Ezra had set his heart on the study and practice of the law of the Lord and on teaching statutes and ordinances in Israel" (Ezra 7:10 NARE). On the basis of the above, the King, Artaxerxes, permitted Ezra to go and "instruct those who do not know these laws" (Ezra 7:25 NARE).

Teaching is thus considered as a necessity for imparting wisdom of God in the Old Testament. A teacher is herein understood to be one who imparts wisdom in addition to having knowledge of the law of God. How the necessary wisdom is imparted can be viewed from several perspectives. Ezra could have been expected to go as an instructor with clear communication skills, as a motivator through his own oratorical capabilities, or as a dramatic performer resulting from his habits and personal living dispositions. Teaching can hereby pass for the work of a teacher seen from Yount's pedagogic lenses as a "dynamic synergist," whereby many elements work together in unison. This synergy is boosted by the fact that the teacher knows God's work well and has been given the ability to teach others, as a gift from God. In the New Testament, we hear the great commission by Jesus Christ Himself: "Go make disciples of all nations … Holy Spirit: teaching them to observe all that I have commanded you" (Matt. 28:19–20). There is yet another instance when He instructed: "And you also testify, because you have been with me from the beginning" (John 15:27). The importance of teaching is reinforced by the fact that the Holy Spirit gives it as one of the foundational gifts to the church for the edification of individual members as well as to the church as an organism. Thus Christian education emphasizes the primacy of teaching as often illustrated by the call on teachers to work with the divine teacher since they cannot attain the goals on their own power. All perceived categories of participants in teaching, namely parents, the church, and school teachers must implore the power of the Holy Spirit to rain down God's power on them to enable their human efforts at making disciples of those they teach.

God's own Initiative

Christian teaching, as we know, operates at the level of whole life. In this scenario, it can as well be defined as discovering God's ways of working and working with Him. In her book, *Education That Is Christian*, Dr. Lois E. LeBar describes teaching as an art. She goes on to state in a very positive manner, showing that teachers are called to work with the divine teacher as they "cannot bring about results in their own power"[27] regardless of the depth of their knowledge or skills. "The Holy Spirit works in the teaching-learning process by inspiring the teacher through the word, through other spiritually gifted believers and leading the heart of the learner."[28] Thus, teaching, she thereby argues, becomes an art where, by the power of the Holy Spirit, the teacher weaves together the interest of the learner, other Christians, and the Bible. We have already affirmed that a great deal of biblical reference to teaching, as shown earlier, adheres to the goal set by Jesus Christ when He said to Peter and company: "Follow me and I will make you fishers of men" (Matt. 4:19 NARE). That was, in effect, "I will make you like Me!" Because Christ was indeed the fisher of men, and it could not mean anything different given His statement: "Everyone who is fully trained will be like his teacher" (Luke 6:40). That further explains why much of Christian education is concerned with helping people to know what their teachers know and as well helping them to become what their teachers are. It also emphasizes we cannot limit the concept of teaching to the formal, traditional perception of knowledge transmission. Teachers train, show examples, influence, imitate, groom, supervise, approve and disapprove, fish for men, make disciples, nurture, and so forth. They are charged in several ways by the master teacher like: "Whatever you have learned or received or heard from me, or seen in me—put into practice. And the God of peace will be with you" (Phil. 4:9). St. Augustine simplified it with the echo: "We speak but it is God who teaches."

Teaching as an Art

In the same frame of reference, Jay Parini, in his book, *The Art of Teaching*, states that nobody simply walks into a classroom and begins to teach without some consideration of self-presentation which he calls a "teaching persona." He then declares: "Teaching can therefore be seen as a conscious art of self-creation, as self-performance. Authenticity was a fiction, and any attempt to communicate to perform a self in public, entailed taking on a mask, a covering. Without the mask in place, there was nowhere for the 'voice' to go; it had to speak through something. It needed the mask as a poem needed line, a play the stage."[29] He then went further to explain that the teaching persona is not a simple process as "it involves artifice, and the art of teaching is no less complicated than any other art form. In most cases a teacher will have a whole closet full of masks to try on for size."[30] And I beg to add—at appropriate occasions. This is in tandem with the Christian education broad definition of teaching.

Teaching and Learning

It is worthwhile noting how teaching that is Christian concerns transformation of Christians into Christ-like individuals bound for heaven. A teacher in this context teaches himself and also teaches others to teach. Simply—it is self-creation as depicted above. Christian educators who are, by their calling, theologians, theoreticians, teachers, and trainers who aim at creating others to become like themselves, must put on the right "mask," which in this case is their exemplary behavior as believer-priests aspiring to make disciples or performing as "fishers of men." It is important to know that Jesus's disciples adhered, with their lives, to the instruction and practice of their teacher. In the Introduction to his book, *Conversations with a Diverse Group of Great Teachers*, Bill Smoot says, after interviewing several teachers over the years, he saw qualities their teaching all had in common: "One commonality is that they all regard teaching as not a job but as a calling, a combination of serious purpose and sacred commitment to the purposes. Teaching is more than what they do; it is who they are, and it defines their place in the world."[31] It should therefore not be surprising when students mimic their teachers positively or even imitate them to the point that they adopt a nickname gleaned from something about the teacher they admire. We should also note that in Christian education, being a continuous learner is one of the attributes of a teacher.

Parini puts it as follows: "The essential journey in this profession is toward self-knowledge; this will involve getting lost in order to get found, losing your thread, having to revise your sense of reality over and over, frequently adjusting to new information, new contexts."[32] In order to stay abreast with the times, the teacher continues to place himself at strategic position to filter life events, knowing he has to have the accurate information and knowledge about the subject he teaches to remain not only relevant but also credible.

Teaching Triad

Smoot went further in the concluding page to embellish the teacher's work in this manner: "Teaching is also miraculous in that someone did not understand, and then the teacher came; something passed between them, and that someone does understand. The teaching triad is the daily miracle: teacher, student, and that which passes between them."[33] This miracle worker must have certain qualities that the average observer can relate to, but most often the teacher is defined from a very narrow gauge, which successfully diminishes the importance of this call. Given that Christian education derives its authority from Scripture, which is the Word of God written in human language, it is appropriate to take our bearing from the characteristics stated therein. Jesus Christ said: "No disciple is superior to the teacher; but when fully trained every disciple will be like his teacher" (Luke 6:40). In view of this superiority, the attributes associated with teachers as provided in Scripture should be an obvious benchmark for determining the direction forthwith. A few citations which are not necessarily exhaustive of available examples are:

1. They are filled with the Holy Spirit (Rom. 12:7; 1 Cor. 12:28–29).
2. They are versed with God's Word (Ezra 7:6; Col. 1:28; 3:16; 1 Tim. 2:7; 2 Tim. 1:11; Titus 2:7).
3. They are enabled to teach others (Exod. 35:34; Eph. 4:11–12).
4. They realize and understand that their ability to teach comes from God and not of themselves (John 7:16–18; 2 Tim. 3:16).

5. Their teaching brings life (Prov. 13:14).
6. They are aware of resistance, dissent, and attacks from learners/subordinates (Matt. 23:34; Acts 4:18; Titus 2:7–8).
7. They are filled with integrity while avoiding pomposity (Matt. 22:16; Titus 2:7).
8. They are not in competition for status with anyone (Matt. 22:16).
9. They are meant to glow (2 Tim. 3:10).
10. They should desire to uphold the truth for all and should illuminate or exude light (Matt. 5:14).

Teachers' Ability

The traditional restrictive definitions of a teacher and teaching simply portray the teacher as someone in a classroom where he/she rattles out content for learners to assimilate with the purpose of having the ability later to regurgitate content at a time of evaluation. This perception has prompted different attempts at improving learning and teaching to the extent that the quality of teaching/teachers has undergone numerous evaluation processes. This ranges from investigation into teachers' backgrounds with respect to the pedigree of colleges and universities attended to pedagogical training attained. Most often, consideration is not even given to the teacher's intelligence and knowledge about the pupils, creativity, humor, understanding of immediate needs vis-a-vis societal issues, commitment and dedication, and belief in the learners' ability. Very little thought has often been given to what indeed are the satisfaction and rewards the teacher garners from his/her profession! Teacher evaluation debate, which has been on the front burner for a while, constitutes another angle to the crisis in the definition of leadership. Several initiatives have been made in different school districts and states in North America to find a working solution in the past several years, given that the Carnegie Institute in Washington, DC, hosted a forum of practitioners and policy makers in 2012 to discuss the challenges and controversies that were seen to suffocate teachers' performance. Blame thrown around the subject ranged from the lack of capacity to conducting effective evaluations to inadequate communication between those evaluating and the teachers who were being evaluated. While the teachers, on one hand, don't recognize the competence of those sent to evaluate them, the evaluators themselves, on the other hand, think the teachers were simply stonewalling. This little sound bite tells much about the level of confusion surrounding what a teacher's job description really is. As long as teaching remains ill-defined, success in evaluating teachers will not be guaranteed. I submit and posit that a quicker solution can be found if a rethink is made regarding the concept of teaching, particularly in line with Christian education principles with a view to realigning teaching with leadership. The result of this narrow perspective therefore appears to justify any argument for the need to return to the biblical root in line with Christian educational concepts and the church ministry education benchmark for future quality evaluation of teaching/teachers.

Contradictions, Convergence/Confluence

Teaching should therefore be referenced from diverse platforms, inclusive of elements, which perceive it as a vocation, a calling, a gift, modeling, an art, a profession and a teacher as a designer, revealer, motivator, communicator/storyteller, trustworthy partner, guide, and so forth. One very good position was presented by Jason Kamras, National Teacher of the Year in 2005, when he stated: "Excellent teachers can make a dramatic difference in children's lives. In fact, I believe that teachers are the locus of power in the fight to close the achievement gap."[34] In addition, he stated that the teachers who are successful at closing the achievement gap "do exactly what all great leaders do when they face seemingly insurmountable odds."[35] In this same line of reasoning, Max De Pree made a prominent notation about teachers when he referred to eminent leaders who contributed to the growth of a specific organization and said: "In every case these people have been outstanding teachers."[36]

In July 2018, the Teach for America (TFA) editorial team enunciated: "Teaching is a demanding role that requires incredible organization and time management skills, as well as the ability to cultivate others' strengths, to persevere in the face of countless obstacles, and to build relationships-the same skills and experience needed to lead within a variety of contexts."[37] In their explanatory discourse, they wittingly paralleled teaching characteristics with those of leadership in what they termed "Four Ways That Teaching Enhances Leadership Skills." Permit me to paraphrase them as follows:

1. Teachers start by developing a strong vision for their class. One of the primary aspects of leadership is having a clear vision, and teachers seek tremendous input from stakeholders—students, families, fellow teachers, and the broader community just as great leaders do.

2. Teachers take strategic actions to reach their vision every day. Since leadership maps out strategy to reach their vision, teachers create lesson plans and prepare assignments to reach their vision.

3. Teachers are adept at building relationships across lines of difference. Teaching offers the unique opportunity to build relationships with a diverse group of faculty, staff, and parents with different backgrounds, experiences, and strengths.

4. Teachers continually push themselves to learn and improve. Leaders learn from mistakes, seek feedback, and continue to evolve, and similarly by nature, teachers are at the center of this kind of culture of learning.

In their review of the TFA impact on the overall society who may have pursued other careers and have worked with leaders from numerous backgrounds, they stated thus: "These leaders all draw on the leadership skills they honed in the classroom." In other words, while they were grooming their skill in teaching, they sharpened and developed their leadership capabilities.

Another dimension being pursued within the public education environment is Teach to Lead, an organization that shines a spotlight on teacher leaders–Advancing Teacher Leadership. Rather than regarding teaching as an element of leadership, a new perspective is being formulated, whereby it is promoted as more of an appendage. To provide the overall picture of this new dimension, I find it will provide clarity to reproduce some sections of the remarks of the then US Secretary of Education, Arne Duncan, given on March 14, 2014, at the National Board on Professional Teaching Standards and Learning Conference held in Washington, DC. While referring to America's teachers and school leaders, he expressed interest in the positive effect on students' successful performance on academic achievement and closing of perceived academic gaps. He admitted that this pronounced success can be attributed to teacher leadership to which he lamented as not having been given the recognition it deserved and thus noted: "According to a new poll, 69 percent of teachers feel their voices are heard in their school, but only a third feel heard in their district, 5 percent in their state, and 2 percent at the national level."[38] One therefore begins to wonder if leadership could be construed by mere recognition at whatever level imagined. Is simply getting some recognition or accolade the sum of leadership? The answer seems to lie at a remote perception and proposition we may need to discern from his subsequent expression. The fact that teachers have contributed immensely to the change in academic achievement, which has resulted in higher standards obviously involves leadership. He then later introduced a caveat when he said: "But the only way that higher standards, and new systems of support and evaluation, will work, is if teachers lead this change in partnership and collaboration with principals, parents, and communities.

Teachers have spoken eloquently about how important it is to have a voice in what happens in their schools and their profession—without leaving the classroom."[39] He then went on to define what he considers is leadership in the context of closing the academic achievement gap by stating thus: "Teacher leadership means having a voice in the policies and decisions that affect your students, your daily work, and the shape of your profession. It means guiding the growth of your colleagues. It means that teaching can't be a one-size-fits-all job—that there must be different paths based on different interests and you don't have to end up with the same job description that you started with. It means sharing in decisions that used to be only made by administrators, and the best administrators know they'll make better decisions when they listen to teachers."[40]

Convergence/Confluence

From the above, we are thrown back to what I had earlier referred to as the human-centered approach as opposed to organization-centered. As if he was making an attempt at filtering the dual approach, and to emphasize the distinction, he added:

> But I can tell you that teacher leadership doesn't mean: clerical or administrative work with a pretty title, counting books or setting schedules. It's not about managing projects and initiative in which you have no say. It's not about a rubber stamp to ideas that have already been decided. It's about your voice, your vision, in the life of

> your school, the work of your school system, and the shape of your profession … members are recognized as experts and leaders in matters of policy. That needs to happen much more in teaching.[41]

In a nutshell, one can discern from this discourse a move in the direction of Christian education path to teaching and learning. He then expressed his optimism about the future with respect to understanding the broad definition of teaching as follows: "Changes happening today I believe—because I've heard it from teachers—that the next stage is about unprecedented opportunities to innovate, to be creative, to focus on critical thinking and problem solving-the exact things that teachers tell me brought them into this profession."[42] Good thinking, one may say, but teachers are rather concerned today with some unity of purpose.

It is common knowledge that teachers have constantly engaged in the call for standardization, which is not necessarily because of a lack for collective knowledge or ability, but for a lack of collective vision and will. In this age of high volume and velocity of information, there is a serious disturbance in the grasp of knowledge such that catching up has become elusive. As a result, the cry for standardizing of what should be taught in schools has assumed a wider scope in order to reduce the unsettling effect of the heavy current of information flow, especially since we cannot control time, nor can we apply some brake to it. The situation thus calls for adjustments in our educational policies to cope with the new age, especially with reference to why we teach. Christian education, however, provides for a focus on the human person with an understanding of a lifelong learning ethic as well as concern for other people. In this way, we are virtually programed to stay on course, in line with the foundational purpose for which we teach. Education must be centered on the student as a person in transformation toward Christ-likeness, through which every other thing may follow. So, focusing on the intellect or book knowledge alone should be regarded as delimiting since this cannot provide for a full identity of the human person. The student should be equipped with deep learning, and social and spiritual maturity in the process for wholesomeness. This translates, therefore, to a call for a shift in the present achievement paradigm where test scores serve to prove learning in itself, rather than evidence of learning and should seek to promote education that will present and showcase who (the student) and not what (the material learned). Here is where rethinking teaching pops up again and which, of course, is partly my argument with regard to the definition of leadership, given that someone had once called for the need to teach holism and depth.

The cardinal base/pivot of teaching in Christian education is the affirmation that it is a gift of the Holy Spirit in which the receiver is graced with innovation, creativity, knowledge, and the ability to deal with immediate needs of the learner while conscious of the future and its potential problems. The teacher continuously prepares against what may be expected in order to retain credibility, a critical attribute of a leader. Smoot, who we had referred to earlier, asked a famous author, Hannah Riley Bowles, what are the keys to your success as a teacher? Her answer to the question was: "I prepare really hard. I put a lot of effort preparing, but preparing in itself is not enough. I really care about communicating them in a way that is interesting and engaging—where smart people will find them interesting and stimulating and relevant to their lives. I care a lot about that. I ... adopting materials that display a broad array of leadership examples demographically; they imbibe the idea that this could translate into being a leader."[43]

This last position of Bowles obviously pushes teaching into an interlocking relationship with leadership such that the elements of each can pass for the other. Given this scenario, it is proper to delve into what foundational examples Jesus Christ, our master Teacher, established. However, a review of our claim He is the master Teacher can be justified with a few illustrations that certainly prove He was a teacher. These scriptural proofs are just a few I like to mention and are not necessarily exhaustive:

> You call me Teacher, and Lord, and you are right, for so I am (John 13:13).

> This man came to Jesus by night and said to Him, "Rabbi, we know that you are a Teacher come from God, for no one can do these signs that you do unless God is with him." (John 2:2)

> If I then, your Lord and teacher, have washed your feet, you also ought to wash one another's feet (John 13:14).

Therefore, whoever breaks one of the least of these commandments and teaches others to do so will be called least in the kingdom of heaven. But whoever obeys and teaches these commandments will be called greatest in the kingdom of heaven (Matt. 5:19).

I will instruct you and teach you in the way you should go; I will counsel you with my eye upon you (Ps. 32:8).

But the helper, the Holy Spirit, whom I will send in my name, he will teach you all things and bring to your remembrance all that I have said to you (John 14:26).

Now He was teaching in one of the synagogues on the Sabbath (Luke 13:10).

Come O children, listen to me. I will teach you the fear of the Lord (Psalm 34:1).

And what you have heard in the presence of my witnesses entrust to faithful men who will be able to teach others also (2 Timothy 2:2).

Teach me the way of your statutes; I shall keep them with care. Give me understanding to keep your law, to observe it with all my heart; I have more understanding than all my teachers, for your testimonies are my meditation (Psalm 119:33).

These illustrations should allay any fears or doubt about the fact that Jesus taught and did so masterly. But what did He teach?

Content of Christ Teaching

It is easy to understand the content of what Jesus taught because it was strictly centered on the human person either as an individual or corporately —the church as an organism. The emphasis was always on human growth in loving the Lord and others, obeying God's Word, doing good deeds with spiritual priorities as first priority, praying, having faith in God, serving God and resisting temptation, and living out spiritual virtues like honesty, mercy, forgiveness, righteousness, humility, purity, compassion, and generosity. And above all, living by the truth. Jesus modeled the elements of teaching as Zelznick beautifully showed by itemizing those that can be best paraphrased as doing the following:

1. Asked questions more provocatively;
2. Answered questions more thoughtfully;
3. Lectured truths more effectively;
4. Told stories more captivatingly;
5. Presented Scripture more enthusiastically;
6. Gave facts more picturesquely;
7. Involved students more meaningfully;
8. Illustrated truths more colorfully;
9. Quoted Scripture more knowledgeably
10. Applied truths more specifically;
11. Met students' needs more definitely;
12. Helping and testing students more compassionately;

13. Corrected students more firmly;
14. Related truths more personally; and
15. Modeled truths more consistently, and so forth.[44]

Robert Pazmino wholly supports the position of Christian education and affirms the belief in the concept—Jesus Christ as the Teacher come from God—with a purpose, example, or model for teaching, having illustrated the same in the way He lived while here on earth (notwithstanding the brevity) and worthy of emulation. His redemptive mission as the Son of God reinforces His distinguishing mark as a teacher. In contrast, He transcended cultural barriers that separated the society of His time, which prevented Gentiles, women, children, so-called sinners, foreigners, and other people groups from access to knowledge acquisition within the new life being offered. Guided by the purpose of making new disciples of all mankind, He exhibited principles that are agreed to by other authors such as Herman H. Horne, Roy Zuck, and others. These principles can be categorized in the following manner:

1. Authoritative that can be referenced to scriptures (John 14:23–24).
2. Rooted in the truth so that hearers can draw their own personal conclusions (John 6:60–69).
3. Thought-provoking to activate and reflect life realities.
4. Lived what He taught through actions even to the point of laying down His life as a demonstration of His love for His friends (John 13:12–17, 31–35).
5. Emphasized relationship with one another, further manifesting love.

These authors unanimously recommend that today teachers take their bearing from Jesus's teaching. Equally, the four Gospel writers (Matthew, Mark, Luke, and John) portray Jesus each from a different but unique perspective of a great teacher. In Christian education, we posit that every leader must know how to teach and is invited to model their teaching after that of Jesus for the transformation of man with the help of the Holy Spirit. It appears, though, that after two thousand years man still finds it difficult to process what Christ taught. When we talk about God in whose image man is created, we deal with relationship and unity in diversity—a reflection of ever-changing multicultural society. In all these, we are called to share in the divine nature through love. Christian education is poised to bring this understanding to the fore by way of leadership/teaching.

So far I have tried to establish the source of Christian education's position with respect to leadership vis-a-vis teaching. It may be interesting to ask: Is it safe to compare the meaning and understanding of teaching in the way the master Teacher demonstrated with our behaviorist writers' formulation, which is often based on observation of animal behaviors? Or, do we fall back to cognitive theorists who centered their understanding of human learning as the acquisition or reorganization of mental structures for processing and storage of information? Given that teaching cannot be divorced from basic human interactions, research into whatever will help x-ray and expose the passage of knowledge from the donor to the receiver would most likely alter the definition, often based on the result obtained. New discoveries through science and technology are certainly likely to provide dimensions, which will fuel diffusion in our perception of what teaching should be, thus creating further disconnect with leadership where it rightfully belongs as shown in the Scriptures.

As Vanessa Rodriguez submits in the Introduction to her book, *The Teaching Brain*, "The key is however that both actors—teachers and learners are equally important to the transfer, understanding, and creation of knowledge and skills. As the process and development of teaching become professionalized, in more formal settings, suddenly the entire premise of the interaction ceases to be a natural interplay between the teacher and the learner. Inside school walls and pedagogical training, teaching is often understood and practiced as if it were a one-way street, with a mostly unidirectional focus on the learner…. the teacher is always down played or overlooked entirely."[45] In order to balance the equation which seems to have lost one half of itself, the focus then shifts to finding a new approach to the position of teaching and the teacher in the process of transferring knowledge. While the struggle for a way forward rages along, redefining the concept of leadership brews, and it becomes possible to resurrect the expectation that it is the function of leadership to improve the overall progress of humanity. That remains the constant. But in Christian education, that happens to be the foundational goal with emphasis on spiritual maturity toward Christ-likeness. However, human systems have, through generations, lured society into focusing simply on result-based leadership whose aim is just the bottom line in today's world. The struggle appears to now shift to reconciling human development for societal prosperity, though theoretical, with workforce satisfaction, which represents practicality. Teachers stand to manage the trade-off between achieving the mission and satisfying today's human daily needs. Regardless of the level of disconnect, leadership combined with its element—teaching—will allow the re-linkage of prosperity and productivity in human affairs.

CHAPTER 5

MIDWAY POSITION AND BYSTANDERS

W e have dealt extensively with how famously difficult it has been to define leadership as to be generally acceptable. In order not to get lost in the morass of defining leadership, given the fact that few people quibble over definitions, we cannot lose sight of the fact that a large number think of leadership as the process of influencing a group toward a defined outcome. This ultimately suggests a single person herds a group toward some goals and that the leaders "craft and direct those end points," otherwise called goals. General Stanley McChrystal, outlines in his *Leaders: Myth and Reality* that when the above common understanding of leadership is held against the reality of how leadership actually works, "three myths are revealed:

1. The Formulaic Myth—in our attempt to understand process, we strive to tame leadership into a static checklist, ignoring that leadership is intensely contextual, and always dependent upon particular circumstances.

2. The Attribution Myth—we attribute too much to leaders, having a biased form of tunnel vision focused on leaders themselves, and neglecting the agency of the group that surrounds them. We're led to believe that leadership is what the leader does, but in reality, outcomes are attributable to far more than the individual leader.

3. The Results Myth—we say that leadership is the process of driving groups of people toward outcomes. That's true to a point, but it's much broader than that. In reality, leadership describes what leaders symbolize more than what they achieve. Productive leadership requires that followers find a sense of purpose and meaning in what their leader represent, such as social identity or some future opportunity."[46]

The author then notes that the power and prevalence of this mythology of leadership tend to rival those of religion or romance and that these myths seem universal and inseparable from our existence as human beings. They also show a disconnect between how things should be and how we find them in practice, yet knowingly live with this disconnect. This confirms that at the turn of each corner, we are led to a more confounding situation.

Regardless of what general or central definition we choose, my concern here is with the biblical concept of leadership as affirmed by Christian educational endeavors toward the transformation of life into Christ-likeness for man's salvation. Some authors, like Joseph S, Nye Jr., have made efforts to simplify the issue when you see the Preface to his book, *The Power to Lead*, as he states: "I define leaders as those who help a group create and achieve shared goals. Some try to impose their own goals, others derive them more from the group, but leaders mobilize with three key components-leaders, followers and context in which they interact."[47] This reduces leadership to a term loosely used and deemed to be understood in varied conversations. But this doesn't quite go down well in situations where leadership and teaching are structurally separated, like in school management where school administrative activity in a formal school environment is perceived as separate from classroom teaching. School administrators are considered to be those involved in leading as opposed to teachers who are mainly associated with pedagogical activities. Results of most research in teacher leadership is perceived traditionally as a theoretical construct, the focus of leadership squarely rooted in the school principal. Cherubini, in his paper, *Grounded Analysis Theory*, notes: "Although there exists a rather voluminous collection of research in the area of teacher leadership the overt emphasis rests on formally recognized positions of additional responsibility and to a lesser extent on classroom teachers. Dimensions of leadership are however, seemingly ignored in the context of beginning teachers"[48] In one analysis of a research study, it was discovered that new teachers were unable to even see themselves as recognized leaders in the school community. Activities they performed daily actually involved elements of leadership of which teaching is prominent and represented leadership influence they manifest. It is rather interesting that the word *leader* itself is ingrained in the culture of education such that only those in administrative duties are considered leaders, which is certainly an exclusive right of the chosen few at the top of the education hierarchy. To corroborate this innate culture, Marilyn Kutzenmeyer, in her book, *Awakening the Sleeping Giant: Helping Teachers Develop as Leaders*, she states: "Empowered teachers bring vast resources for continuously improving the schools. By helping teachers believe that they are leaders, by offering opportunities to develop their leadership skills, and by creating school cultures that honor their leadership, we can awaken this sleeping giant of teacher leadership." As obviously designing a "peeling-off" as this appears in leader/teacher relationship, the author went further to tell a reviewer that which can best be illustrated in his own words: "As we were writing the first edition of this book, we were counseled by a reviewer of a draft manuscript not to use the phrase 'teacher leadership'; but simply talk about teachers, because she believed that teaching is inherently a leading profession. However, we held on to our notion that using the term teacher leadership helps teachers develop new ways of viewing themselves, their roles, and their profession."

You can see the depth of the culture discussed earlier. And to crown that feeling, it is worthy to take note of their (Kutzenmeyer et al) definition of teacher leadership in the final analysis: "Teachers who are leaders lead within and beyond the classroom, identify with and contribute to a community of teachers, learners and leaders and influence others toward improved educational practice."[49]

Should it appear so complex a system to understand leadership as presented? I don't think so. A similar example can also be drawn from the public setting when we look at Teach to Lead, an initiative of the National Board of Professional Teaching Standard, ASCD and the US Department of Education. The program aims at advancing student outcomes by expanding opportunities for teacher leadership. It is said this would be achieved by providing resources, facilitating stakeholder consultation, and encouraging professional collaborations to develop and amplify the work of teacher leaders. In short, the crux of the culture we are alluding to is vividly captured in the program's mission statement, produced verbatim as follows:

"Teach to Lead envisions a world in which teachers are valued as the foremost experts in instruction and as such, are leaders in developing, informing, and implementing education policy and practice to steer systemic improvements to benefit student learning."[50]

To achieve the objectives they listed follow-up actions that include, among others:

1. "Increase pathways and opportunities for teachers to exercise leadership;
2. Elevate teacher voice to inform and develop policy and practice."[51]

This position clearly produces two camps in the system that place teachers, the experts, now to be nominal leaders (teacher leaders) while the real known leaders maintain their post. Nonetheless, all hope is not lost in this ever-changing scope of leadership in its concept definition. Brad

Lomenick presents a remarkable bend to the Christian education position in his *Catalyst Leader* by providing what he calls eight essentials for becoming "a change maker." He starts by perceiving leadership as influencing, making a difference, leaving a mark. The typical nexus with the Christian education narrative comes in the fact that his eight elements are rooted in the belief that they are God's gifts. "As God unfolds the possibilities and opportunities sitting at our fingertips. May we not just lead now, but lead well"[52] He further advances that in order to be an influencer, eight elements must be all present:

1. Called—You therefore need to find/discover your uniqueness;
2. Passionate—Live in pursuit of God;
3. Authentic—You should be able to unleash the real you, thereby avoiding faking;
4. Capable—Make excellence non-negotiable;
5. Courageous—Prepare to jump;
6. Principled—Anchor in your convictions;
7. Hopeful—Build toward a better tomorrow;
8. Collaborative—Draw power from partners.

An interesting and relevant exposition Lomenick also provided in the appendix of his book is the result of a study in 2012 by his organization in partnership with Barna Research Group on "Today's Christian Leaders." In a nationwide online survey of more than 1,000 Christian adults (eighteen and older), respondents chose what they consider to be the most important traits that leaders need to possess, given all the changes taking place in the world.

Ten different options with specific meanings were given as follows:

1. "Courage—being willing to take risks;
2. Vision—knowing where you are going;
3. Competence—being good at what you do;
4. Humility—giving credit to others;
5. Collaboration—working well with others;
6. Passion for God—loving God more than anything else;
7. Integrity—doing the right thing;
8. Authenticity—being truthful and reliable;
9. Purpose—being made for or called to the job;
10. Discipline—the ability to stay focused and get things done.

The results showed that of these ten characteristics listed, most Christians believe integrity is the most important for leadership today (64%). On the next tier are authenticity (40%) and discipline (38%), which are followed by passion for God (31%) and competence (31%). The least important features are purpose (5%) and humility (7%). Vision (26%), collaboration (25%) and "courage (15%) are ranked in the middle of the pack."[53]

What I consider of interest in the results and relevant to us is that *purpose*, which is said to mean "being called," is actually recognized as a gift of the Holy Spirit. One can see that today's adults would rather not bother as they perceive it more from the point of view of a *job description*, thus focusing on an organization bottom-line approach as against human quality and growth. The corroborative effect of teaching being a gift and regarded as an essential element of leadership appears clearly unnoticed or simply undermined. Scriptural presentation of teaching as a gift appears rather farfetched.

We need, however, to note that "All scripture is breathed out by God and profitable for teaching, for reproof, for correction, and for training in righteousness" (2 Tim. 3:16). We are equally reminded elsewhere: "One who is taught the word must share all good things with the one who teaches" (Gal. 6:6).

Detaching Teaching from Leadership

It is reasonable to argue here that due to the practice in the real world, apparently to appease society, the tendency to detach teaching from leadership, as we have seen in most of the writing so far, is very high and can be argued as simply to create new avenues for professional endeavors. In some cases, they are so separated that one may not find any relationship whatsoever of one to the other. To have a meaningful discourse on this issue, let's first see who the Bible identifies as teachers—they were either individuals or groups with unique traits as leaders. A few will suffice here:

Priests—"And you must be able to teach the Israelites all the statutes and ordinances that the Lord has given them through Moses" (Lev. 10:11). Moses—"At that time the Lord charged me to teach you the statutes and ordinances for you to observe in the land you are about to cross into and possess" (Deut.4:14).

The Apostles—"The apostles gathered together with Jesus and reported all they had done and taught" (Mark 6:30).

Fathers of children—"However, be on your guard and be very careful not to forget the things your own eyes have seen, nor let them slip from your heart as long as you live, but make them known to your children and to your children's children" (Deut. 4:9).

Fellow believers—"I myself am convinced about you, my brothers- that you yourselves are full of goodness, filled with all knowledge, and able to admonish one another" (Rom. 15:14).

Nicodemus—"Jesus answered and said to him you are the teacher of Israel and you do not understand this?" (John3:10).

Gamaliel— "I am a Jew, born in Tarsus in Cilicia, but brought up in this city. At the feet of Gamaliel I was educated strictly in our ancestral law and was zealous for God, just as all of you are today" (Acts 22:3).

Having identified some of the teachers, it is pertinent to also remind ourselves that they were leaders as well in their own right. Where leadership is perceived differently from teaching and vice versa can only be found in secular literature and academic construction and often in practice due to the inexplicable reason of separating one from the other as different functions. A worthwhile and significant setting can be located on the use of the word *discipling*, which is the pivot of the biblical commission to go make disciples of all nations. While scriptures provide the message as shown earlier in the Introduction, the practice out there in the real world has morphed into virtually all manner of interpretation in order to appease or correspond with societal thinking and evolution.

Biblical Characteristics of a Teacher (Leader)

Nonetheless, the biblical meaning of a disciple or those who can be called disciples have these characteristics:

—Followers of Christ as against followers of Moses (John 9:18).
—Someone of good works and acts of charity (Act 9:36).
—Some to act as witnesses in Jerusalem, all of Judea and Samaria and the ends of the earth (Acts 1:8).
—Those who bear much fruit to glorify the Father (John 25:8).
—Those who take up their crosses daily and follow Jesus (Luke 9:23).
—Those who imitate Christ (1Cor. 11:2).
—Those who do not look out only for their interests but also to the interests of others (Phil. 2:4).
—Those who are trustworthy (2 Tim. 3:2–7).
—Those who are disciplined (Heb. 12:11).
—Those who can renounce all they have including their lives (Luke 14:26–32).
—Those who show love for others, that is, one another (John 23:34– 35).
—Those who train people to renounce ungodliness and worldly passions, and to live self-controlled, upright, and godly lives in the present age (Titus 2:12).

The list continues throughout the Bible, paying attention to particular circumstances. There were occasions Jesus warned against false teaching (1 Tim. 6:3–4) as well as against hypocritical teaching (Rom. 2:21). As we have said earlier, the central focus is that Jesus said the result should be that the pupil, when fully trained, should become like his teacher. We are further shown that you do not detach teaching from leading since, after all, teaching will not stop until the day we see Jesus face-to-face: "No longer will they teach their neighbor, or say to one another, 'Know the Lord,' because they will all know me, from the least of them to the greatest." So, it could as well not be too much from this revelation to speculate that teaching transcends leadership.

Experience—A Prerequisite for Leadership/Teaching

It is important to pay attention to the high premium the Bible places on experience with respect to teaching and leadership ability. It is categorically stated that no one who is a recent convert be appointed to the position of leadership. Regardless of the level of your experience in your previous profession, you would not have had the privilege, if you like, of mixing freely with those who had associated directly with Jesus or his disciples, or of having been tested and seen to have imbibed the group culture, a necessity for the ability to transmit or pass on the message to others. Certain catch words and phraseology are employed by the authors to project the emphasis—entrust, imitate, acquire wisdom, being tested, model, love, and so forth. They usually connote specific cultural meanings, which would certainly not be familiar to outsiders. Ashira Prossack of

Forbes Women, a Millennial and Generation Z engagement expert and speaker, corroborates this view when she wrote about communication skills required by a leader: "Without a high level of communication skills no leader will truly be successful. He will be able to clearly express himself and therefore lead with greater clarity. He must be familiar with listening, advising, directing, motivating, teaching and coaching to understand that different situations call for different communication styles and be able to switch between them with ease."[54]

Experience provides room for acquiring wisdom, and it is often advised that wisdom garnered from experience should not be ignored. Having been close and working with the present generation, which I will call the "New Age," Lomenick utters his regret in their effort and culture of diminishing the importance of experience: "Sadly, few leaders today are tapping the great well of wisdom found in a mentor. According to one research, only 16 per cent firmly assert that they interact regularly with an older mentor who helps them navigate professional issues. Too many young leaders think they know more than their elders."[55] Failure to admit the existence and impact of experience on the ability of an individual to perform doesn't by any stretch of the imagination render it ineffective. The practice of making reference emanates from the general recognition of someone's past experience. Even in the secular society, an employer would often seek background information about a potential hire prior to bringing such a person on board. Most recruitment application forms have provision for references. That depicts a direct affirmation of the importance of experience. In Christian education, every leader as we saw from the requirements must be tested first before engagement, and a substantial part of the requirement needed to scale through is the ability to teach to ensure the continuity of the group/organization, that is, being able to pass on the baton. Teaching ability in its dynamic synergism will always provide that threshold and the importance attached to it.

Being Called and the New Age

Young Christians of these days do not even consider the idea of "being called" to any role they find themselves in as of any significance. A job is good so long as it can pay your bills at that moment and as time progresses. If and when your bills increase beyond what the current job can pay, you need no soothsayer to inform you of the need to seek out another, better-paying job. Besides, nobody in his right senses would want to stay in one job for a decade no matter the calling. God forbid. We are then left with a question if calling is a lifelong affair. If that is the case, it then translates to a life sentence to poverty since it is generally believed any employee who becomes a millionaire must have stolen from somewhere or done something illegal. Being called, therefore, if it exists at all, must be from season to season to suit the new age if it really has a place. This has forced the experience requirement for job seeking to diminish in importance given the philosophy of the new age, which is often proudly articulated thus: Experience simply helped to solve problems of the past or related present, but the position being sought requires the ability to deal with future problems, which are not likely to be similar to those of the past and present! The training I received, some would say, does not expect me to memorize the multiplication tables when calculators are littered everywhere. It does not require any experience to use new or updates apps and computer software programs but, rather, being computer literate to the level of required usage! Moreover, you can always update your knowledge by online certification! The new age interprets calling not as a hidden treasure one must search out in remote far-away places. It is not buried deep beneath an unmarked ground. God has placed it in plain sight where it is easily identifiable and accessible as well. The important code is the willingness to learn. While writing this book, I had the opportunity to watch a TV program on the ABC 13, network showing one of the 2019 graduation ceremonies at the Coretta Scott King Young Women's Leadership Academy in Atlanta, Georgia. Each of the graduating seniors, when interviewed by the presenter, referred to their operational policy of "Continuous Learning Dreamer," which they believe will carry them through life as they move into the world of uncertainties. They echoed their having been trained to be leaders and that one sure way of becoming a leader is by maintaining the culture of learning on a daily basis, believing in your ability to succeed by refusing to listen to those who remind you of your limitations. You should rather know that you can learn what you don't know, insisting on seeing yourself succeed, and getting an outsider to see you as you see yourself. A new mantra is "As I see *me*." This tends to capture the direction of the new age where leadership no longer requires a ladder or scaffolding to climb up, no waiting for your turn or getting equipped and being prepared now for the future. You can simply learn anything from YouTube. The path to influence has been truncated thus, yielding a clear circumvention or even a total scrapping of what used to be known as the proper or normal channel. TV fame, stardom, celebrity mentality, success in response to the dictates of the internet, social media trending, and any digital footprint are now what matter. Social media "followership" has assumed primacy such that it threatens or rather equates with leadership in status, and it can be achieved in mere minutes or even seconds.

Growth & Maturity

Issues bothering on growth, physical or mental, are no longer in sync with maturity. These have all been overtaken by sophistry of location or clime, culture, religious orientation, gender option and choice, and so on. Growth is now better defined by savvy in technology, skill, or as manifested through performance. Nobody waits any longer for time in order to grow into anything, as technology has equipped the new age for instant leadership since they have created their new platforms for determining the new mode of doing things.

Teaching, like leadership, appears also in jeopardy. Gerontology and its derivatives are no longer suitable in the lexicon, and we should note that those we often idolize are humans like the rest of the population. Equity has been reconstructed and brought to focus, the need to know that life is really no longer a "series of blocks laid earlier on," and one's twenties would not "establish one's seventies" as perceived by the Lomenicks of this world. It is now only apparent that life should only move in one direction—forward. The new age doesn't have the patience to listen and take notes. They would rather take snapshots or video clips. In the same way, nobody would want to carry cash to go shopping when drones can now deliver to any destination in the heat of online shopping. Robotics are replacing messengers, self-driving vehicles simply need updates of apps and software, and no one cares for mentors any longer.

Lomenick depicts it as: "Part of technological effect on leadership is that it doesn't always allow us space to incubate and mature as individuals and as leaders."[56] The position of writers in the mold of Smoot is frustratingly cast out of the window given his statement: "As a teacher you have to joy in guiding students to change and grow. You have to be enthusiastic about the student's improvement. Or if they're not yet, you have to be honest—some things are going to take a long time." This stand is certainly perceived as archaic and obsolete and cannot be tolerated in the new age. It vehemently contradicts the instant opportunities to grab information very readily available on the internet, YouTube, social networks, and so forth that are immediately accessible on the smartphone. Karen Tye gives a beautiful description of the situation as she stated the following in her *Basics of Christian Education: "The* tyranny of the urgent … I think we are a culture addicted to the urgent."[57] As earlier stated, this deals with the loss of patience in the way the new age is carrying on in life. The culture is evidently entrapped in the urgent, thus constituting a hindrance. If something appears not to work now, it is considered not real, and the tendency is to discard it and move on to the next new idea. In a real situation, one is expected to exercise due patience which is tantamount to steadfastness—a virtue often required in teaching and in leadership as well, and usually emphasized in Christian education. It does not, however, stop at being patient. A leader must learn to listen to his followers because if you want to change the world, you must first be able to listen.

Contradictions about how leadership should be perceived are as numerous as definitions offered by various writers on the subject. The decomposition of leadership into distinct human activities like political, military, business, labor, civil rights, sports, academic, social, and so forth tend to present leadership as determined by such activity. These activities lead to group formation with varied goals to reflect their particularity and peculiar goals, yet are considered appropriate for the respective body, and if stretched further, would evoke the need for a unique kind of leadership to enable them to actualize their goals. Expectation of what the leader should be doing equally becomes dispersed across the varied composition of the group, notwithstanding the crafted goals. Providing an encompassing definition of leadership to capture the array of group expectations becomes not only ridiculous in conception but simply not prudent. Our sense of leadership from Christian education and as provided by scriptures offers a unifying frame of reference as well as unity of purpose.

Leadership in Church Community

> "And he gave some as apostles, others as prophets, others as evangelists, others as pastors and teachers, to equip the holy ones the work of ministry, for building up the body of Christ, … we should grow in every way into him who is the head, Christ, from whom the whole body, joined and held together by every ligament, with the proper functioning of each part, brings about the body's growth and builds itself up in love.
> (Eph. 4:11–16 NARE).

> The church as revealed to us by Jesus Christ Himself constitutes the gathering of people in His name: "For where two or three are gathered in my name, there am I in the midst of them."
> (Matt.18: 20 ASV)

In human affairs and development, the family avails the first opportunity for education. Christian education wholly embraces this philosophy and therefore continues to incorporate the participation of parents who provide a foundational leadership and teaching framework (a miniature church) for an individual. Leading and teaching at this stage is so intricately weaved that one is perceived as the other in all practical terms. Deuteronomy 11:18–19 then reinforces the coupling as: "You shall…therefore lay up these words of mine in your heart and in your soul, and you shall bind them as a sign on your hand, and they shall be as frontlets between your eyes. You shall teach them diligently to your children and shall talk of them when you sit in your house, and when you walk by the way, and when you lie down, and when you rise."

Teaching is therefore not only regarded as transformative in Christian education but is understood to be a process that continues along the growth of the individual through life. The obvious participants in this call must play their roles at appropriate level in the life of the individual. Pope John Paul II stated it this way: "The Christian family constitutes a specific revelation and realization of ecclesial communion, and for this reason too it can and should be called 'the domestic Church.' All members of the family, each according to his or her own gift, have the grace and responsibility of building, day by day, the communion of persons, making the family a school of deeper humanity."[58] The church community, having recognized its origin from the family, promotes the faith journey, which requires educating the whole person, given his nature as a human being. The Old Testament clearly illustrates the fact, given that there were no formal schools where children could be taught, parents were obligated to pass on their knowledge of God through teaching and an exemplary life. The master Teacher, Jesus Christ, reconfigured the setting in the New Testament by introducing the element of truth and widened the scope to accommodate children, women, and even those labeled "sinners" by the early teachers. In her effort to lead the fallen man back to his Creator, the church embraced the new direction by putting emphasis on providing a solid foundation in view of the lifetime growth required within the process. Leaders in the church are chosen from those who are able to know the truth and are well able to teach as the church represents, as it were, a distinctive community within the society and culture. The church is equally structured in such a way as to provide a socialization setting for all aspects of personality in the growth process for both the individual members as well as the church in its corporate form as an organism.

Christian education endeavors to locate leadership and teaching roles within the church setting as designed by the response Christ gave to James and his brother John when they requested seats on the table, one to the left and one to the right as recorded in Matthew 20: 27 "Whoever wishes to be great must first be a slave." That completely negated the secular concept of what leadership was known to be and set a new trajectory for educating, ministering, and making disciples. Leadership was given a new color. In his blog, Mike Ayers gives the imagery in this form: "People are of immense value to God, more important than anything numeric or material; biblical leadership takes place in the context of Christian Community. Jesus didn't simply tell the disciples to show up at the temple and there lecture them on principles of leadership; Jesus did live with those he led. He chose to impart himself, not just his teaching."[59]

Leadership in Stewardship

> "And what you have heard from me in the presence
> of many witnesses entrust to faithful men who will
> be able to teach others also" (2 Tim. 2:2).

Leadership in stewardship is targeted at ensuring continuity and aimed at saving the future, as believers mature physically and spiritually. One critical skill required to ascertain the achievement of the set goal is teaching. Henry Brooks Adams puts it wisely: "A teacher affects eternity; he can never tell where his influence stops." As we probe into the subject of stewardship, we are immediately charged with the duty of being conscious of accountability, and if there is a break in communication, that duty suffers seriously. Christian education uses scriptural phraseology and refers to teaching as a gift of the Holy Spirit, and we are invited to utilize the gift in serving one another as good stewards of God's varied graces. It thus remains incumbent on us as teachers and stewards to carry out our leadership duties as required, bearing in mind the Christian concept of servant leader as against the master-servant posture of the secular world. In this instance, the leader/teacher bears the burden of being the custodian of what needs to be handed down and must do so with utmost care. A leadership movement— The Catalyst—established with the objective to help produce and inspire the next generation of leaders, coincidentally goes along the same message by their approach: "Being a catalyst leader, means you are working to identify, understand, and pursue God's unique call on your life with passion and patience."[60] It goes on to advise thus: "Every leader faces a temptation to project a persona rather than be themselves. They think that in order to maintain the confidence of their team, they must appear faultless, flawless, and ever wise. Yet most organizations need an authentic leader, not a perfect one."[61] This illustrates and projects the color painted with a Christian education brush. It is also corroborative of what Christie Caine, co-founder of the AZI Campaign, stated: "There is beauty in imperfection. When something becomes too polished, it loses its soul. Authenticity trumps professionalism."[62] A leader and a teacher are both perceived as models in their expected duties, and this is affirmed by Scripture. "Urge the younger man similarly, to control themselves, showing yourself as a model of good deeds in every respect, with integrity in your teaching, dignity" (Titus 2:6–7 NARE).

Leadership in Worship

> "So what is to be done, brothers? When you assemble, one has a psalm, another an instruction, a revelation, a tongue, or an interpretation. Everything should be done for building up" (1 Cor. 14:26).

The leader must ensure orderliness when the community is in worship, which by itself demonstrates peace as well as the presence of God. Given that our faith leads us to love and worship God, it stands obvious that our behavior should mirror our transformational endeavor as well as our resolve to stay the course. Christian education places a high premium on informal teaching (the invisible curriculum), commonly known as body language. When a teacher is teaching and at the same time exemplifies what he says by what he does with enthusiasm, it certainly portrays an act of worship. That reinforces an expression of God's presence, which, after all, is all that matters. Being passionate constitutes an element of leadership and when deployed, regardless of where you work, it is equally an act of worship. It is clear that leaders who exhibit passion for God will in all probability have a positive influence and impact on others. This corroborates the scripture verse: "Whatever you do, work at it with all your heart, as working for the lord, not for human masters" (Col. 3:23 NIV). In worship, the leader must provide the proper atmosphere for members to utilize their varied gifts for the growth and edification of each individual member as well as the group in a corporate form. Thus the leader's heart becomes vital to being a change maker vis-à-vis an influencer. Worship provides congregational gatherings needed for each other, which reflects the true meaning of worshipping God. Leadership is promoted and structured in that context.

Leadership in Service

> "Since we have gifts that differ according to the grace given to us, let us exercise them; if prophesy, in proportion to the faith; if ministry, in ministering; if one is a teacher, in teaching; if one exhorts, in exhortation; if one contributes, in generosity; if one is over others, with diligence; if one does acts of mercy, with cheerfulness"
> (Rom. 12:6–8 NARE).

Leadership in service calls for excellence in what we do and particularly what we pass on to the next generation, knowing that today's habits constitute tomorrow's culture. Leadership, which really is teaching by way of modeling, mentoring, and serving by exemplary behavior, encapsulates what the scripture features as service. A writer I admire, Ken Blanchard, once said: "Leadership is a process of influence. Anytime you seek to influence the thinking, behavior, or development of people in their personal or professional life, you are taking on the role of a leader." So when we serve with a sincere heart, we are exhibiting character which Christian education holds as its flagship value. And in *Catalyst Leader*, referred to earlier, Lomenick insists: "The depth of your character determines the reach of your influence."[63] Inasmuch as from time, most societies accord genuine respect to leaders, often interchanged with teachers in meaning, not only because they were the only people around who had steady jobs and income, but also because of their display of character. It turned out to be a position any forward-looking parent would aspire to for their children. As the master Teacher, Jesus so demonstrated when He washed the feet of His disciples and noted: "If I then your Lord and Teacher have washed your feet, you also ought to wash each another's feet" (John 13:14 NARE). To corroborate, Scriptures provide yet in another verse: "Make my joy complete by being of the same mind, maintaining the same love, united in spirit, intent on one purpose. Do nothing from selfishness or empty conceit...Have this attitude in yourselves, which was also in Christ Jesus" (Phil. 2; 2–5 NARE).

At community service and worship sessions, teachers are seen playing leading roles and physically engaging in routine duties serving in furtherance of program direction. Such prominence in participation reinforces the symbiotic nature of leadership with teaching in a practical form and validates why they are used interchangeably for same meaning. In concluding his book, Lomenick leaves the reader with what I consider should be a chorus for leaders/teachers: "The time has come for you to be what God has called you to be, to live out His purpose for your life…As you pursue this calling, make excellence a nonnegotiable. God deserves your best… And finally, don't believe the lie that you are the center of the universe. Seek out older leaders who can help you, and guide you. And then pour out your life into others."[64] This clarity simply prompts our thinking into making disciples of all people.

Leadership in making Disciples

> "Go therefore and make disciples of all nations,
> baptizing them in the name of the father, and of
> the Son, and of the Holy Spirit, teaching them to
> observe all that I have commanded. And behold,
> I am with you always until the end of the age"
> (Matt.28:19–20 NARE).

Scripture provides that leaders must be able to teach and should not be recent converts, among other qualities. One other dimension Christian education emphasizes is the duty of a learner to graduate and become like his teacher— the hallmark of making disciples. Both requirements are necessary for nurturing to spiritual maturity in the journey toward Christ-likeness. They are expected to replicate themselves for continuity such that at some point, the teacher would pass for the leader and the leader for the teacher. This is in tandem with the commission and would happen given the assurance that the Lord is always with us. It also shows clearly that you cannot lead if you do not know how to teach, and to be able to teach, you must have been in the group long enough to understand what has been commanded. Christian education takes cognizance of this and hence affirms that teaching is multifaceted and not simply a transmission of book knowledge from teacher to learner. It becomes clear also that experiential knowledge through immersion, imitation of the model or mentor, evaluation by testing, and various character formation blueprints must come to bear in making a disciple. From this dimension, leadership appears clearly as a position of influence or a set of personal characteristics formed over time. And it quickly rules out the idea that "leaders are born and not made." It shows also to be in sync with the Christian education view that discipleship results from transformation. Besides, if someone is born a leader, he would have no need to be taught or even learn from someone else. It indirectly reinforces the notion that the ability to teach is a gift, an element of leadership. It registers with our conviction that the church is an organism designed by God for the purpose of evangelizing and making of disciples. Christian education helps to shape the strategies and approaches to ministry, which facilitate the transformation process. In this entire setting, teaching assumes the posture of an art where, by the power of the Holy Spirit, the teacher weaves the interest of the learner, other Christians (the church), and God's grace to propel the human efforts at making disciples. As we have noted earlier, teaching is perceived and practiced in the secular academic environment from a decomposed and fragmented approach so far away from mentoring, exampling, guiding to stimulate spiritual growth, leading, and so forth, which all contribute to making disciples for Christ.

The Culture of Fragmentation

Christian understanding of the process of spiritual growth of the individual as well as the group, which we in our everyday conversation refer to as the Christian Community, is in a disturbing decay. As already presented in this book, growth in this perspective means transformation toward Christ-likeness while *community* in the context is the broad scope perceived as a combination of the process of building a community of two or more people bonded together by a commonality, and being in a state of oneness. The word *community* is prominent in Christian education in the same way as *leadership* and has as well been bastardized through the culture of fragmentation, such that its meaning has become vague and most often confusing. For clarity, fragmentation can be described as follows:

I.   The action or process of breaking something into small parts or being broken up this way;

II.   The process in which an organism breaks into different parts with each part growing into a complete new organism;

III.   The situation in which a formation, be it an industry or social/business activity, breaks into many units, but none is more than the others.

Fragmentation provides room for one to see the world as constituted by things rather than processes. Separation, for example, simply and quickly becomes fragmentation and even isolation in a snapshot. It has generally been noticed that in our present world, the forces of industrialization have become essential forces of fragmentation and are leading to a path, based on the primacy of the parts rather than that of the whole. Fragmentation, if not checked, is progressively but gently destroying humanity. The rush to specialization with its consequential competition feeds fragmentation to the extent that a sense of unity is fast becoming an abstraction. The feeling of "them as against us" continues to grow as the norm. In an organization, there is greater competition between those within versus those external, who ought to be the real competitors. While corporate managers square up with frontline counterparts, marketing department managers are in combat with several fronts, such as manufacturing and procurement. In various aspects of life endeavors, disharmony and discord appear to be at the forefront of events leading to constant demand for separation, division, and even isolation. In the process, there comes the weakening, waning, and oftentimes secession of basic commonalities which result in fragmentation of community expectations. As would be anticipated in our present multicultural society, which we often express in positive terms that the world is becoming a "global village," the necessary unifying factors do not seem to appear on the horizon. Directly and somehow seemingly in reaction to this situation, Keith Tester, in his review of Zygmunt Bauman's article, "Seeking Safety in an Insecure World," notes a "secession of the successful" who have become wholly detached from any and every community such that they have become "incapable to understand why others want or need it." He then portrays how Bauman "sees men and women lining themselves up to be next for destruction at the hands of globalization." He foresees the inability of those who have succeeded and seceded to help in promoting a community where we can accept that "we are all with and for one another regardless of the signs of local affiliation."[65] The challenge we all now face is the need to retrace our steps to the truth about God's original design for creating us and at the same time providing three pillars for growth or transformation toward likeness of Christ. These support pillars or elements for growth include community, relationship/friendliness and neighborliness.

Community

The Merriam-Webster dictionary defines community as: A unified body of individuals: such as a group of people with a common characteristic or interest living together within a larger society; a body of persons of common and especially professional interests scattered through a larger society; a body of persons or nations having a common history or common social, economic and/or political interest.[66]

A Model of Christian Community

This is predicated on a commonality of faith in Jesus Christ, the Son of God by a group of people who have been saved/initiated through baptism and belief in God, agreeing to share a common faith in Jesus Christ, the only begotten Son of God. Having been born anew, they are willing to live a life of purity and truth and to follow the new nature that embraces love, compassion, relationship, and unity kindled by the Holy Spirit who illuminates and sanctifies individual members as well as the group. The unitary aspect of community in the Christian model is based on commonality of our roots as children of God through His Son, our common transformative journey, and common relationship/bonds of friendship as equal members of the church as stated in Ephesians 4:1–6. The concept of community in Christian education is predicated on the performance of a communal activity by the community of faith for their benefit and that of the society. It is tuned permanently to the channel that sings, "That they may be one!" It does not call for a recalibration of society to install community thinking and feeling but rather to show the light and attract the people to follow, to be salt of the earth, and to lead in breaking down the invisible boundaries between the "us" and "them."

Notwithstanding that the word *community* has been corrupted and rendered somehow vague and confers no specific target in meaning, users of the word still produce varieties of collectives to suit their envisaged purposes. It can, therefore, be applied to a region, nation, the world at large, cities, and villages. Some create a double-barreled mask like household-community, city-community, medical-community, and so forth. The critical fact worthy of note is that when applied as a stand-alone, it elucidates a very broad scope in definition, which often leads to confusion. In social science literature, writers often do not struggle to define the word *community* but would rather describe it as a common understanding of a concept associated with certain elements combined in a set, which often include locus, joint action, social ties, and sharing of actions for achieving a purpose. A well-known author, Chavis, D.M. et al., presented it as elements which, when combined, give a sense of community involving membership, integration, influence, emotional connection, and fulfillment of collective needs.[67] In today's multicultural society, these core elements are applied to wield or create any group, such as sociocultural, political, sexual orientation, and so forth, to forge out a community where the group is known to be consciously seeking unity for a purpose. It usually works out well in a cosmopolitan environment. The dynamics of today's practical world is a good enabler for laying emphasis on any given element, such as locus (what may provide a sense of "my place") in a specific geographical location: street, town, city, zip code, village, and so on. It may equally involve a specific setting like a community building, school, workplace, church, and even organized zonal meeting areas. Some need for a joint action can foster an instant formation of what can pass for community, for example, contributing to a common course, such as advocacy, organizing to recover from the pains of a catastrophic event, or a push for collective betterment. Diversity provides a strong platform for demographic and social differences in age matters, race, socioeconomic status, gender and sexual orientation, profession, and such groupings of divergent purposes. Chavis shows the importance of the membership element as it functions as the spirit of belonging together, a feeling of mutual benefit of being together, thus creating emotional safety. It alludes to "cognitive dissonance" associated with the members' willingness to sacrifice on the community's behalf. In the Christian education environment, this aligns with the central theme of Romans 12:5: "So in Christ we who are many are one body, and each member belongs to one another." It parallels with several other verses in the Bible, such as the following:

> Do you not know that your bodies are members of Christ? (1 Cor. 6:15).

> Now, you are the body of Christ, and each one of you is a member of it (1 Cor. 12:27).

> Therefore, each one of you must put off falsehood and speak truthfully to his neighbor, for we are members of one another (Eph. 4:25).

The echo that emanates from membership can be ferocious in impact on the target, since it appeals to the emotional level and can be quite penetrating, given that it is centered on what is believed to be the "truth" within the group. The first task of the community is to always tell the truth to one another, and this trades on the psychological as well as the emotional courage of every member, which can be traumatic if the truth is not forthcoming. Faith is established between the member and the group with mutual trust that each party wants and cares for the other at critical moments and so cannot afford to be found wanting. Humiliation stands by as a consequence for corruption of truth of the group, that is, the community.

While the second element—influence—puts members in a position to make sacrifices when due, acceptance into the group assures members of the group's backing since the boundary between "us" and "them" has been effectively broken. The third element provides order and peace, both of which supply necessary oxygen and energy for exercising authority, which then confers power to the community for creation of social rules and norms. The rules and norms build up the capacity of the community for the failure of growth, which can augur chaos and ultimate ruin.

Reacting to Christian church perception of community, author James Estep Jr. in the book he edited, *A Theology for Christian Education*, says: "Our fundamental concept of community is likewise a reflection of the Trinity since not only do we bear his image individually but also corporately. Community implies more than relationship, for it also includes a sense of community and a unity in the midst of diversity."[68] In relation to membership, which we saw earlier was given primacy amongst three elements, James posits as follows: "Christian education takes a community approach toward its participants. This is due especially to the reality that is created through God's work of adoption and the believer's union with Christ and baptism with the spirit. The new reality that results from these particular acts of God in salvation is a Community of Christians joined together as brothers and sisters in the family of God and as members of the body of Christ, the Church."[69]

Other Christian writers refrain from conjuring situational need to carve out a community or to create one through symbolism. Lawrence O. Richards presents it from an in-church peer group experience and posits thus: "The

Christian Community is a community of those who share faith's life. While parents may be the primary models for their children, additional models are important as is the development of a community which mirrors and reflects faith's life."[70]

Imagined Community

Still talking about writers' position on community, Benedict Anderson's book, *Imagined Communities* (1983), was widely hailed as a new political perspective on the topic–community. The idea grew into a new concept of nationalism, which could urge a collection of individuals and groups to aspire for a nation if there exists a commonality of that aspiration. In a review of the book Max Bergholz stated: "He provided those seeking to tell histories of nationalism with a new conceptual vocabulary to execute and explain human agency, and specifically the role of imagination, in the making of nationalism into a real political force."[71] Meanwhile, Bergholz pointed out in his review that Anderson himself maintains: "I propose the following definition of the nation: it is an imagined political community, and imagined as both inherently limited and sovereign. It is imagined because the members of even the smallest nation will never know most of their fellow members, meet them or even hear of them, yet in the minds of each lives the image of their community."[72] So within this parameter, human circumstances can cause creation of communities no matter how temporary they may be. Imagined community concept appears to have influenced another perspective illustrated in the heat of a protest action against the construction of a dam somewhere in Australia, where the leader of the movement orchestrated a community to fight their cause. It eventually emerged as a symbolic politics of belonging and thus–a community. This was particularly concerned with the amalgamation of interrelated issues of belonging, community identity, and social diversity which were negotiated into a commonality of interest. The group borrowed the idea from Abner Cohen's argument on symbolic politics, a term in political anthropology, in which he asserts: "Under certain structural circumstances some interest groups which cannot organize themselves as formal associations manipulate different forms of symbols in order to articulate informal organizational functions. Everywhere, Man the symbolist and man the political act on one another. Often, different forms of symbols are exploited to achieve one organizational function and one form of symbol is exploited to articulate different organizational functions."[73] This explains why the campaign succeeded, given an unusual alliance of farmers, environmentalists, urban retirees, some Aboriginal people, and others of complete divergent backgrounds and interests.

Community Existing in Memory

It is interesting to note a unique and recent view by Chris Arnade in his recent work, *Dignity* (2019), in which he shows that what used to be known as community is eroded, in other words, gone and only exists in distant memories. Something like community is something about the past: "They are left with a world where their sense of home and family and community won't get them anywhere, won't pay their bills."[74] It is also perceived as being in the same boat or caught in the same weird situation when he says: "In this Bakersfield neighborhood, those using drugs are very much a community, with the McDonald's one of their club houses. They almost all know one another, almost all help one another out, almost all swap info on housing, drugs, and the police. They bond over shared experiences of trauma, pain and isolation; they also bond over a belief that life is bleak. So bleak that the ultimate downside of their situation- death- isn't terrifying."[75] By the foregoing scenario, we are once more exposed to the fundamental questions about social inclusion and exclusion, particular versus general interest, and identity and belonging, associated with the concept of and sense of community. Anthony P. Cohen's theory of symbolic construction of community, with its emphasis on the appearance of similarity among differentiated members as opposed to assumptions of actually shared meaning, systems, and interpretations, is practically demonstrated here. This seems to be in contrast with Graham Day's view of community in his *Community and Everyday Life*, in which he is interested in the impact of newcomers on established population groupings, in how boundaries are drawn to include and exclude, and in how circumstances can change the intensity of people's sense of belonging to community. Recognizing that the reality of community is a great deal "messier" than most theorists wish to acknowledge, he seeks to avoid dichotomous contrasts between "simplistic polar oppositions."[76]

The Genealogy of Community

Since the Bible says we are created in the image of God, it would be correct to infer that God created us for community. This is anchored on the doctrine of Trinity, which shows that God Himself is community. We need not go too far to prove otherwise, given that the creation story began with, "Let us make man in our image" (Gen. 1:26). Man must therefore have been wired to long/aspire for community, which is part of God's image of which we are His bearers and which quickly syncs with Christ's redemptive sojourn on earth to redeem the fallen human. The expansive work includes restoring humans back to the image of God with inbuilt capacity for community. The focus of the work of transformation cannot be accomplished without community involvement. It is most unlikely that we can become what God created us for outside of community, in view of the nurturing nature of a community. The sense of one-another rule availed by community provides for creating, redeeming, and transformation.

In Summary from the Christian Education Perspective

Community should not evoke the fear it tends to when it is unwittingly associated with communal life of early Christians. Rather, it is God's purposeful design for growth. Christian community is simply a platform for sharing a common life in Christ. It transcends mere social contacts with persons outside an isolated private life. The biblical community is more of a challenge to us Christians to pursue a life, which can easily be perceived by observers as encapsulating the people of God from their individual lenses as well as corporate. A community posture offers room for growth in love because it is already evident that love of oneself is innate. Within a community, there will be a variety of opportunities to foster the mission—to love one another as you love yourself, teach and encourage each other, pray for one another, and so on. The emphasis is on *one another* and does not necessarily mean living together under one roof. It borders more on unity of purpose with one spirit, one mind-set—in Christ. It is a template for continuing nurture and transformation to spiritual maturity toward the fullness of Christ (Eph. 4:11–16).

Community provides the forum to appreciate the presence of Christ in our midst by way of the forgiveness He gives us as we forgive those who trespass against us. There is hardly any other practical way to demonstrate this invocation without a sense of community. In the same frame, when you confess your sins and you are forgiven by your brother or sister, all share in the healing work of Christ.

Community promotes guidance, learning from each other while ensuring accountability or stewardship as known in Christian environs. It confronts the individualistic idea of the "mind your own business" lifestyle, which stifles growth while promoting mediocrity. It allows for continued evaluation through healthy comparison in line with maturity in transformation toward Christ-likeness. A modeling mold is found in Ephesians 2:12–13.

Community involves a place to pray and worship: "Where two or three are gathered in my name, I am in their midst." When we assemble to pray and worship, we adhere to the instruction to pray for one another (Eph. 6:18; Jas. 5:16). Confessing your sins cannot be a lone star exercise but surely requires one another. It is often said that the community is at its best when it provides and promotes prayer and worship.

Service can only be possible in a community as Christ always taught that He came not to be served but to serve. Service in this context conveys scuttling self-interest, forfeiting pride and arrogance, and promoting humility. John 13:2–10 recounts Christ washing the feet of His apostles; we learn and practice the art of serving and beyond to include the beauty of giving not only material things but sincerely pouring out love through caring.

Community Impact

A shining example, the Christian community manifests by its character and action, the light the world needs in order to follow Christ. We are sent to be models of what God wants for everyone, that is, as light of the world, salt of the earth, those whose lifestyles reflect that of Jesus so as to confirm that He was sent by the Father, and are people who live by the truth. It is a community that radiates compassion, kindness, and love in contrast with the world of deceit and wickedness surrounding them. Community offers opportunities to exchange creativity in putting to use their varied gifts and talents to honor each other in individual and corporate edification, promoting truth in reality without employing deceit and lying for convenience (Eph. 4:25; Col. 3:9).

Community provides avenue to show compassion and love by initiating one form of support through missions for feeding the hungry, praying and healing for the sick, accommodating the homeless, legal aid and counseling, direct evangelism, and so forth.

Community provides a base for forging relationships while maintaining vocations, family structures, and social engagements. We are strengthened and enabled to carry on with our lives without disruption. Community kindles continuity of life and generational growth.

Christian community holds the flag of invitation for those not yet convinced or who may be confused as to their future faith journey. A call to community rekindles the spirit of God's purpose that man was not created to go through the world alone. Happiness is best realized beyond singularity. The simple statement of Jesus—come, follow me—depicts the call for community, a community comprised of different people from all parts of the earth, who shall love God and one another and be able to pass on the good news to our friends and neighbors as Christ taught (1 Corinthians 15:1).

Relationships/Friendships

A not-too-popular saying states: "It's not easy to form intimate bonds in today's world—but it is possible."

The natural feeling that there is a resistance to form intimate relationships in today's world may sound like some generalization, but when critically examined, it tends to click in the positive. We are buried in transience brought about by the constant need to move on, either as a result of a search for greener pastures or a call of duty, which may require relocation at short notice. Whatever the reason, it boils down to having to separate from family, old friends, and acquaintances, with the consequence of losing support, bonding, and sometimes protection we value and enjoy while in their company. The change in location may offer a wider scope of contact with the possibility of greater and qualitative opportunities, but for sure, new acquaintances would require time to settle deeply for any meaningful relationship. It is also good to remember the culture of the present age, which rarely believes in staying too long on a job. What is of essence here is that if the concerned individual stays long enough to build new bonds, it is likely that he will absorb some characteristics such as behaviors, response patterns, and feelings of the new community which will remain with him after he separates.

The culture of pursuit for money, power, fame, love, and so forth tend to saddle us with too much baggage, which often leaves us with no room to consider what our priorities should be as each item of our to-do list appears to be so important and necessary and, at the same time, is neglected or kept on the back burner. It does not even occur to us to reflect that the items on such a list are numbered or at least written one after the other in some order!

Natural Instinct to Connect

In Christian education, we recognize that all human beings are created with an innate desire for connection with others.

From birth, the child cries out for contact, and as he/she grows, that instinct grows along, failing which, the quality of life may become dull and questionable. As physical maturity endures, the need for relationship grows deeper to the point of having to seek being appreciated and loved, obtaining affirmation from those around us, and feeling connection even from those in far distant places.

God's design for man incorporates man's happiness, and this depends on man's ability to get along with others. Any relationship, be it family, marriage, community, or general society, presupposes teamwork. God designed man's nature for teamwork, which by a very simple observation, can be seen in our body build, starting with two eyes, two legs, two hands, and so on. We need not forget that God created them to complement each other, and we are alerted to the spiritual pre-creation collective work by the Trinitarian expression: "Let *us* make man in our image." It is no coincidence that this is reported in the very first book of the Bible, Genesis. Teamwork was thus given primacy in man's existence and growth *ab initio*.

Jesus Christ continued to unveil the principle of teamwork in His earthly journey by action like sending out His twelve apostles in their diversity, in twos to mission, through metaphors like when He unbundled the idea of the Church as His Body. Biblical pronouncements about the vantage position of plurality continue to point to the value of teamwork: "Two are better than one, because they have a good return to their labor; if either of them falls down, one can help the other up; But pity anyone who falls and has no one to help them up. Also, if two lie down together, they will keep warm. But how can one keep warm alone? Though one may be overpowered, two can defend themselves. A cord of three strands is not quickly broken" (Ecclesiastes 4:9–12). Among several occasions, such as in Hebrews 13:5, we are informed, "I will never forsake you or abandon you," which fittingly provides a foundational encouragement for teamwork in Christian faith. It is the assurance you are given when you accept Christ as your Lord and Savior, even when you are alone. The model and structure of our Christian approach is systematically illustrated at various points in fellowship, marriage, dispersing of His gifts for edification, and the ubiquitous presence of the phrase, "one another." This phrase is not only featured as significant but is constantly employed to emphasize relationship, unity of purpose, and fused with love in the bond of peace. From simple variations of exhortation, it appears to culminate in: "A new commandment I give unto you, that you love one another; even as I have loved you, that ye also love one another. By this shall all men know that you are my disciples, if ye have love one to another" (John 13:34–35).

The need for Teamwork

We need to understand that although there may not be the express use of the term "teamwork" or "community" in the Bible, the obvious nature of man's physical and spiritual growth cannot progress without their presence. No one can have a successful life in isolation. How do you determine if someone is honest or trustworthy to fulfill the exhortation in Matthew 5:14? Bear grudges in Ephesians 4:26? Forgive others in Matthew 6:14–15? Do to others in Luke 6:31? We do recognize that the Lord often allows people who do not initially appeal to us to enter our lives. As we get better acquainted, we discover attributes or qualities that reinforce or complement us. Sometimes unusual circumstances may bring us together and expose to us the richness of another personality, and we then realize the need to leave our options open with an acceptable attitude so as not to miss such invisible richness. Building intimacy in today's world presents unique challenges with the influx of social networking and digital friendship. Can we really obtain the biblical prescription of relationships? But we need not despair, as our Lord has designed us and people of every age for the joys and struggles of close friendships. The commonality comes from our being adopted by Christ as His brothers and sisters, thus providing a platform for forging ahead and sustaining the relationship by the grace of God.

We cannot, however, pretend that serious problems do not exist in our present materialistic society, especially problems that we don't see and so don't grapple with. Arnade posits: "We primarily valued what we would measure and that meant material wealth. The things that couldn't be easily measured—community, dignity, faith, happiness—were largely ignored because they were hard to see—especially from so far away."[77]

It may be appropriate to sum it up by saying that one single way of having a relationship that can foster a lasting and sustainable friendship is to be able to understand that for a better life, we can do with a little empathy in the way we live and be able to listen to one another. After all, when you listen, your body-control mechanism forces you to remain silent, thus giving the other person the opportunity to speak. A conversation takes place in a peaceful manner. It is no wonder why the words *listen* and *silent* share same letters and number thereof.

Neighbor

Who is my neighbor? We learn that Mosaic laws demanded of the Jewish community compassion and justice be guaranteed to the foreigner because God loves the sojourner (Deut. 10:18). Neighborliness is the center point of all the legislations at the time of this question. It therefore means that the culture in the society was not tolerant of noncitizens. The answer Jesus proffered clearly means that a neighbor was anyone with whom you come in contact—whether Jew, Gentile, or Samaritan. (Luke 10:25–37) From the community reasoning we dealt with earlier, we should be aware of the constant use of the term *one another* when dealing with the subject of love, compassion, relationship, and neighborliness, as we all belong to same community, given the bonding in Christ.

The meaning of the word *neighbor* tends to appear intricate, especially when viewed from different classifications and even derivatives of its stem such as neighborly, neighborliness, neighborhood, and so forth. In order to avoid the complications that may arise in the pursuit of an acceptable definition, we intend to focus attention in the

Christian education concept as perceived in the question, "Who is my neighbor?"

Before yielding to the biblical context in the answer given to this question, it is useful to consider how relevant the concept *neighbor* is in a society that values individualism, self-reliance, and even upward mobility. It even lacks a place or simply fails to fit into the normal social setting classification—a friend, an acquaintance, a soulmate, a family friend, my school mate, a member of my church, a colleague, and so on. What quickly comes to mind when someone introduces another as a neighbor? Do you see him as someone held dearly or just an average acquaintance? How closely? In terms of common usage within a given society? A specific community? In terms of the level of knowledge?

Apart from semantic scrutiny of the word, it can be viewed from a thematic configuration similar to how Jesus put it in the story of the Good Samaritan. One interesting dimension is discerned in a key character, Jeff Sharlet wrote in his book *The Family* is when Pastor Ted asked his staff, "Do you like your neighbors?" And for that matter, "Do you even know your neighbors?" The answer: "Not really" and "No." Ted deduced a few rules thereby: "I want to meet with people I like." That is, he didn't want to be forced into fellowship with people who weren't his "type." Another rule was: "I don't want to study something I am not interested in." His point being that arbitrary small groups would make less sense than self-selected groups organized around common interests. In this frame of reference, *neighbor* attracts no meaning whatsoever![78] What this shows is not only a thematic view but illustrates that words can change in meaning or assumed meaningless as well over time. The conventional definition based on physical location also denotes one who is there for the other or one who helps and serves in good times and bad. Standing on the platform of locus, we may then bring to bear a recent incident in the city of Dallas, Texas, where a neighbor called the police in an effort to seek protection for his neighbor upon noticing that his neighbor's front door was still open at 2:30 a.m., which was, to his reckoning, unusually late. The police arrived, parked their vehicle at a distance, and approached the house stealthily in darkness. On trying to make contact with the occupant while conscious of their own safety, they ended up shooting to death the innocent home owner– neighbor via a window. In this circumstance an act of neighborliness appears to have gone awry, one would think. Playing the devil's advocate, a bystander expressed that if they were actually good neighbors, he should have first given her a call to find out if there was something wrong (assuming he had the phone number) before embarking on calling the police. The caller has confessed the incalculable damage to his conscience in the blame game for trying to save a neighbor. He feels he killed his neighbor unknowingly in some sort of reverse gear! If we restrict the meaning to location with respect to proximity and those who can fill in a need-gap, we are then faced with where to place those who live on other close-by streets or nearby towns or cities. And with the evolution of "friends" within the expansive scope we now have as provided by Facebook, Twitter, various group chatting apps, and other social media outlets, one is tempted to ascribe an equally expanded meaning to neighbor as well.

This expansion in perception tends to be in sync with the purpose of the story of the Good Samaritan as a way to demonstrate how to be neighborly! An expansion of the legal obligation of loving a fellow Jew in line with the culture warranted that only Jews be accorded with such, hence the Gentiles cannot be allowed to enjoy neighborly privilege of which the overriding factor is mercy and compassion (Luke 10:37). Notwithstanding that scripture doesn't say if the inquisitive lawyer obliged to the advice of "go and do likewise," the critical lesson established is the expansion of the scope and meaning of the word *neighbor*. And of course following forth is the golden rule: "Whatever you want men to do to you, do also to them" (Matt. 7:12). Herein the notion of service is introduced in addition to mercy and compassion. And love is essentially a fulfillment of the law as clearly given in Romans 13:9–10; following forth are: don't avenge your neighbor (Leviticus 19:18); let each of us please his neighbor for his good, to build him up (Rom. 15:2); be truthful to your neighbor (Eph. 4:25); Love your neighbor (James 2:8). The main focus is to live a life that will attract others, the unbelievers, to Christ and to become saved, which is the will of God. Given the covenantal mentality with respect to relational and cultural limitations among the Jews, barriers existed by way of grouping society between cleanness and uncleanness. This often revolved around what they interpreted as sons of darkness versus sons of light. There were consequences as well for not obeying the law.

Christ came to expunge the limits so as to delete all boundaries or such invisible walls surrounding humans. He went beyond their imaginations by even including the love of enemies in Matthew 5:43–48. The special emphasis on perceiving Gentiles as neighbors greatly expanded Jewish horizons as had never been conceived. The common language of one another became universal in application by an inclusive mind-set rather than exclusive setting. When therefore talking about love, compassion, relationship, neighborliness or one-of us, we refer to same community with equal belonging with one commonality—Jesus Christ to substantiate the overall purpose: "that they may be one."

The culture of fragmentation has put a wedge between the realization of the purpose for which community, relationship, and neighbor were designed to thrive for human spiritual growth and transformation toward Christ-likeness, which is a serious challenge facing Christian education.

The next chapter will attempt to juxtapose teaching and leadership from the lenses of some notable writers or organizations reflecting their perception of the relationship to each other.

CHAPTER 6

A JUXTAPOSITION

As to the fact that leaders are given the responsibility of carrying out the commission, various theorists and writers have agreed but have gone in different directions to interpret the way to go about it. This highlights the original perception that both the leader and the led are in the same boat, heading in the same direction, with the same spirit to serve, and granted that the purpose remains unaltered nor adulterated. Over time, the purpose evolved, and the invitation to serve in order to be able to arrive fully matured through the process of the journey faltered in its evolution. The student is no longer being expected to become the teacher nor even a teacher. New ideas were invented by way of seeking for goals, vision, objective, innovativeness, passion, and so forth, and consequently were adjudged fitting enough to replace the original God's purpose with the hope and expectation that He will shower blessings notwithstanding. This book argues that the complexity brought about by this evolution has resulted in the derailment of man's perception of leadership.

A well-known author on leadership, Tom Sergiovanni, has recognized this fault line and has provided insight on the need for rethinking leadership as a subject. In a 1992 conversation with Ron Brandt, a leading editor of Association for Supervision and Curriculum, (ASCD), he shared his views by clearly arguing that the concept in itself is not outdated but rather required rethinking.[79] Other notable writers like Lawrence Richards, William Forster, Richard Bates, TFA, Deborah Chang, Joseph S. Nye Jr., and others followed suit to be at the forefront of recognizing that theories enunciated by psychologically-based theoreticians may not after all be as relevant, given that Pavlov, Maslow, Hesberg, and their ilk were simply focused on behavioral achievement and competitiveness, and mainly with animals. It is equally now clear that even leadership and management literature have traditionally been written by men with masculine orientation and imprint. It never occurred to them that women could be leaders, not even recognizing that women are wired in a way that they are more concerned with sharing and community involvement—two salient biblical prompts in the message. Sergiovanni further argued resoundingly that someone can succeed in a psychological sense in leading an enterprise with all leadership skills but without commitments and end up promoting the wrong things.

Figure 1 below presents what some writers posit as characteristics of good leadership, which, in this book, would rather be presented as its elements. The consensus of their inputs align with the call for a need to rethink, using the factors/elements which are common: vision/purpose, communication, trust/integrity, relationship, moral, knowledge, and love. Chapter two of this book outlined a few of these factors, but it will serve well to also review a couple here: relationship and morals.

Relationship

A biblical relationship is rooted in friendship, which in itself is characterized by love, the kind of love that is depicted in the stories found in Proverbs, church doctrine, and the ultimate example given by Jesus Christ. A true friend demonstrates love, shares wisdom, grants forgiveness, and encourages others to promote one another's welfare. In Colossians, we are told that friends also teach one another as they worship God together. With reference to all of the above, any group that places importance to these values would certainly prosper. Relationship therefore remains a genuine threshold for future continuity of a community where there is the conation among members to act on their moral judgments and behave as leaders of character. Teamwork is paramount such that when leaders share their identifiable values and live them visibly on a daily basis, it creates trust, which then welds all participants together as one whole.

It is a known fact that organizations that share values as they carry on their vision are usually effective because the values impact every facet of the system. Due to the relationship attribute, every member exhibits commitment to the corporate vision or purpose. Each member wants meaning in their life beyond their daily routine to the extent that they want to contribute something meaningful. They are willing to go the extra mile due to the love-based culture embedded in the community. It is tacitly agreed that the leader is positioned to play the role for which he is uniquely qualified and not necessarily because he is superior to anyone else. The same reasoning is applied to knowing that each person's unique gift is meant to enable the community's sustenance. It follows that the key to creating a love-based culture is that everyone involved assimilate the culture and own it. In this way, even at the peril of one's comfort or convenience, decisions are strictly aligned to the corporate values. Therefore, the power of brotherly/sisterly love and friendship in the group activity fosters enthusiasm and momentum to push forward, as all are sincerely committed.

Christian leadership perception from relationship is more than a role that is played; it is a reality that is lived. They are truly committed to the goals and values of the group they lead, and their followers are seen to recognize that quality in their leader. Ephesians 4:15 refers to speaking truth to one another in love, which in general includes willingness to be honest with one another even when it hurts to do so. This also leverages on two pillars— intimacy and sharing authority. Intimacy is portrayed by acquiring the ability to know people around you beyond the role they play in the group to their preferences and inclinations. It not only offers a sense of involvement, but also denotes some level of vulnerability. The trade-off is the genuine caring emanating from a friend in such a group where mutual respect ensures seamless corporation. Sharing authority, on the other hand, provides for mutual responsibility. Each member recognizes that what A does echoes what B is doing or would do because they are both co-creators of the ideas to get the system working the way it is designed. Individual decisions are based on shared purpose and mutual commitment depicting each other's thoughts and feelings. It all coalesces in a duty in relationship, which appeals to a good, fulfilling dose of justification in contributing to shared values and purpose.

Oftentimes, the leader's moral authority plays a role in fostering relationship behavioral practice. It is also viewed as a compass for group reactions to issues relating to the need to work together toward the same purpose. Over all, relationship, honesty, and trust weld together to support the inherent collaboration, producing the expected results.

Morals

From the Bible story of creation, we are told that God created man in His own image. It is thus inferred from that image that man is a moral being who can make a choice between good and bad, and is able to differentiate right from wrong. Man's knowledge of God's law provides the template for determining the good from the bad. We are told also that God wrote His laws in our hearts by way of implanting conscience, notwithstanding the fact that we often find a way to distort it to our selfish advantage. Morality is illustrated by the Christian charge to do the following:

- Work diligently as though working for the Lord or as if He is our immediate supervisor.
- Treat others as you yourself would want to be treated.

- Deal honestly in all financial matters.
- Pay your debts, taxes, and render all that is due.
- Ask always: will this conduct encourage others to serve God better or set a bad example?
- Is this conduct consistent with the standards I profess for others to follow?
- Every Christian in a leadership position has the moral obligation to assess his/her conduct against these biblical standards regardless of the organization he/she belongs to. Figure 1 outlines these varied perceptions culminating in broad understanding of leadership.

Figure 1
Varied Perceptions of Leadership

Lens	Source/ Authority	Base/Pillar	Elements as perceived
Christian education	Bible	(a) Leaders (b) A group (c) A goal (d) Method to get to the goal	1. Vision 2. Purpose 3. Planning 4. Action 5. Communication 6. Problem solving, Delegate, Create 7. Rule over 8. Increase by discipleship
Urban Meyer	*Above the Line*	Mind Change	1. Vision 2. Trust 3. Knowledge 4. Creativity 5. Communication

Albert Mohler	*The Conviction to Lead*	Overall change	1.Transfer of conviction 2. Affecting action 3. Motivation 4 Intuitions 5. Commitment
Firehouse	Firehouse website	Overall performance	1. Integrity 2. Initiative 3. Innovation 4. Insight 5. Inspiration 6.Interest 7. Intensity 8. Information
TFA	Teaching as Leadership	Rubrics—Overall change	1. Set big goals 2. Motivation/Trust 3. Vision 4. Evaluate 5. Intensity (work relentlessly) 6. Planning purposefully
Steven Anderson	*Integrated Leadership Systems*	Overall performance	1. Passion 2.Respect 3. Curiosity 4. honesty
Tom Sergiovanni	*Educational Leadership*	Overall performance	1. Norms/ Moral 2. Commitment 3. Professionalism 4. Relationship
Margaret Bell	Chain Reaction Foundation	Overall change	1. Ability to delegate 2. Excellent communication skills 3. Confidence 4. Honesty 5. Creativity

Mike Ayers +	*5 Distinctives of Biblical Leadership*	Overall change	1. Multifaceted, Holistic 2. Calling 3. God–oriented and people–focused 4. Character and Motivation 5. Community/authentic relationship
Brad Lomenick	*The Catalyst Leader*	Overall change	1. Called 2. Authentic 3. Passionate 4. Capable 5. Courageous 6. Principled 7. Hopeful 8. Collaboration
Deborah Chang (Contributor) +	Huffpost (9 Reasons Great Teachers Make Great Leaders)	Overall performance	1. Create 2. Set high expectations 3. Prioritize 4. Plan purposefully 5. Execute 6. Learn constantly 7. Persevere 8. Resourceful 9. Empathize
TFA Editorial Team +	Leadership (Four Ways That Teaching Enhances Leadership)	Overall Performance	1. Vision 2. Strategic Action 3. Adept at building relationships 4. Continuous learning to improve

+ Clearly specified teaching as element that enhances leadership.

Synchronization of Leadership and Teaching

So far we have seen that writers have been converging to affirm the prominence given to teaching in every discourse involving leadership as every position tends to focus attention on teaching to determine the depth of leadership success. A cascade of a few of these positions from notable leaders whose performances are widely attested to, plus ordinary writers/ authors whose opinions have been influential will help here, using their known interesting quotations, and although not from the Bible, they are in total agreement with it.

> A man should first direct himself in the way he should go. Only then should he instruct others. ~ Buddha

> Treat people as if they were what they ought to be and you help them become what they are capable of becoming. ~ Goethe.

> The role of a teacher is a noble calling—a combination of explainer, listener, friend, coach, story teller, and strategist. ~ Dr. Daryl Eldridge

> A teacher affects eternity; he can never tell where his influence stops. ~ Henry Brooks Adams

> To know how to suggest is the great art of teaching. ~ Henry Fredric Amiel

> He who dares to teach must never cease to learn. ~ Richard Henry Dann

> The average teacher explains complexity; the gifted teacher reveals simplicity. ~ Robert Brault

Looking at the master Teacher, you will notice that Jesus created and utilized teachable moments. He did not rely on classrooms, handouts, electricity, or tables to teach the disciples. We shouldn't be tied to them, either. In Matthew 23, Jesus addresses the Pharisees and other teachers of the law with several warnings of special relevance to teachers. These statements, often referred to as "The Seven Woes," paint a pretty ominous picture of what the Lord thinks about those who abuse their teaching position or do not take their responsibility seriously enough.

Unity of Biblical Writers

From the Bible, our source of truth in Christian education, of all the witnesses, not a single one has contradicted the other but rather embellishes or reinforces the message with words more relevant and impactful to the teaching aspect. The leaders who were being sent to deliver the message were thus given clarity—a subtle job description. The language then becomes not only more meaningful but couched directionally. The purpose becomes as glaring as a road map/ GPS for those willing to undertake the faith journey and able to recognize it as such. Notwithstanding your status in the society, no matter the environment, the phraseology suits the circumstance and usually takes cognizance of appeals to the young and old, as well as gender. We are constantly reminded of the need for unity of purpose, given the fact that we are expected to be one family composed of fathers, mothers, brothers and sisters—all children of God bonded by family ties through our love for one another as commanded, and being conscious that the world was populated from the family unit, moving into Church, and then baptized therein, thus being created anew. We were then given a fresh start and taught to reconstruct our perception of new self as children in order to qualify to enter the new earth, recreated as well by the power of the Holy Spirit. It is useful to note here that human research and development (R&D) has not played any role in biblical matters because the world has subtly agreed to its inerrancy—maybe—at least to even try and review and possibly recast the wordings or structure of the message!

However, the biblical directives where teaching is distinctly positioned as an essential element of leadership can be discerned from a verse reported by Matthew and paralleled by Mark: "Go and make disciples of all nations, baptizing them in the name of the Father and of the Son and of the Holy Spirit, and teaching them to obey everything I have commanded you. And surely I am with you always, to the very end of the age" (Matt. 28:19–20). This command also appears in Mark 16:15 as follows: "Go into the world and preach the gospel to all creation." This commission totally depicts the synchronization of leadership and teaching. It doesn't show harmonization, nor blending, nor merging, nor convergence, but reveals how *teaching is an essential element of leadership.*

The key words—Go and make disciples—readily and instantly tell what is expected but don't stop there. To lock it in, it reinforces the command by directly employing—and teaching—them. Note the repetition. The ordinary dictionary meaning of the word *essential* denotes a thing that is absolutely necessary. Something so important as to be indispensable; it belongs to the very nature of a thing and therefore is incapable of removal without destroying the thing itself or its character. It is therefore something that is the foundation without which the complex whole will collapse; something on which an outcome turns or depends. Without even worrying about the content of the message, the emphasis placed on teaching brings out the need to ensure that it be done. As to who was being commanded, it is obvious that the leadership is the messenger in this situation, and we have already seen who they are as well as what their qualification should be. For emphasis, we are referring to bishops, church elders, apostles, teachers, deacons, evangelists, pastors, overseers, and older women members of the church. Richards contributes to this idea in his statement: "Leaders in the church are selected from those who not only can know and teach truth, but leadership requirements focus on the examples they are to provide."[80] So if you occupy any of the positions listed above, then you are a leader in the believer community who would have been tested and found to be humble and gentle, patient and seen to love one another to preserve unity through peace. Within this peaceful community, they live as one under one God who is Father of all and above all and also in all. To add to this relationship and love of one another, Mike Ayers in his blog article "Five Distinctives of Biblical Leadership," defines leadership as follows: "Leadership is an opportunity to bear the image of God in relation to one another. It is inextricably tied to godliness."[81] They are all able to teach just like those who are already teachers among them imbued with the same qualities. Having established the fact that we understand who the messenger in this regard is, we can now take on their portfolio as given:

Teach—we look on leaders to baptize and teach; therefore, a leader should know how to teach and to do so successfully. Such a leader should have accurate knowledge of the commands of Jesus. In Mark's parallel account, he introduces: "preach the gospel to all creation" for which he showed that they "went out and preached everywhere, and the Lord worked with them and confirmed his word by the signs that accompanied" (Mark 16:20 NIV). In other words, results were visible and experiential. This becomes an appropriate point to reinforce that teaching ability is a precondition for any aspirant for a leadership position. It is more than just significant or something that offers an advantage; it is strictly a necessity. It is important to note certain evocative words that persistently pop up in this Great Commission from various gospel writers—Mark, Luke, Paul, and John, which add strength and momentum to the instruction given: share, remain connected, teach the older women, make, come follow me, live, and so on. As Jesus calls His disciples His witnesses, exhorting them to share the things they have seen and heard, the need for experience is brought to the surface for both the teacher and the taught. Richards explains it as: "In Christ, differences of culture, background, race, social status, educational background, age, opinion—even doctrine—are swallowed up in a unity based squarely on relationship with Jesus Christ and mutual sharing in His life."[82] Since someone has seen or heard what they are preaching (experiential knowledge), it is easier to believe him and in what he is talking about. It further reinforces the faith since someone else has shared the gospel. And let's remember here that no boundaries were set, but rather they should reach out to all the earth (world) and all creation, hence no discrimination as to Jew or Gentile.

Go and Make Disciples

This is clear evidence of an instruction issued to someone perceived to be a teacher. A disciple is expected to live according to the teachings of Jesus Christ and therefore is completely devoted to his Teacher. The relationship between the teacher and his student in the discipling process entails more than mere passing of cognitive knowledge. According to Richards, in Christian education, teaching requires that: "We need to be close enough to them (students) for them to see Jesus in us. The withdrawal of Christians from involvement in society, and from close relationships with acquaintances, is hardly supportive of God's purpose in evangelism."[83]

Live

A disciple's life style can be a perfect mirror for a mentee to constantly look into for self-evaluation. So, making disciples goes beyond instructing or telling others. Examples matter for modeling, which we agree is better accomplished through socialization as explained elsewhere in this book. Actions, it is said, speak louder than words. Further expansion of the instruction includes another word: *entrust,* which is done in this form: "And the things you have heard me say in the presence of many witnesses entrust to reliable people who will also be qualified to teach others." Here again is a proof that teaching ability is needed and for the purpose of obtaining experience which in itself is said to be a "good teacher" in a stand-alone context. It equally provides opportunities to delegate and open up space for expansion of the reach of the message.

Share

A perfect sign of love for one another. Human nature has a way of prompting an open mind to share a pleasant experience with others. Philip shared his own experience with Nathaniel when he told him: "We have found the one Moses wrote about in the law, and about who the prophets also wrote—Jesus of Nazareth, the son of Joseph" (John 1:45). What then are friends for if they don't share something they have experienced and derived pleasure from?

Remain Connected

Jesus said He appointed His disciples on His own volition. He chose them and not the other way round. He certainly knew those that would bear fruits that would last. His purpose for choosing them, as He emphasized, included the need for them to remain connected to Him—the Vine. Being part of the body requires performing the assignment to enable the advancement of the kingdom. This will be done by teaching. "From the whole body, joined and held together by every supporting ligament grows and builds itself up in love, as each part does his work" (Eph. 4:16). Richards adds his sense of this: "If all that is done by the gathered body focuses in a coordinated way on the Person of God, praising Him and lifting up His Person, an exciting new awareness of each individual's identity as part of His people is fostered. And the vertical as well as the horizontal dimension of the Christians relationships is affirmed."[84]

Come, Follow Me

Being called affords them the opportunity to deploy their skills already acquired from their previous professions to the new assignment in order to be able to do things they may not have imagined. Experience is played up once more, remembering that at least seven out of the twelve apostles were fishermen who were now called up to be fishers of men. We cannot therefore shelve or shove off their experience, which will now be needed in their new career that will require teaching and preaching. The issue of preaching is better illustrated by the stress on the word *proclaiming.*

Proclaiming

When you proclaim, you beam light on a specific subject or a definitive message. It is more than a mere announcement. It is stating a fact like John the Baptist did when he proclaimed the imminent coming of the *one* who will baptize with the Holy Spirit. The activity of John in announcing the coming of Christ is proclaiming. Jesus's activity in announcing the reign of God is also a proclamation as stated in Mark

1:14–15: "After John had been arrested, Jesus came to Galilee proclaiming the gospel of God: This is the time of fulfillment. The kingdom of God is at hand. Repent, and believe in the gospel." It is a corollary to witnessing, which is really an attestation of facts of the physical experience of an event or an occasion. A public affirmation by word or example. Similarly, it is stated in Acts 28:31 that Paul "proclaimed the kingdom of God and taught about the Lord, Jesus Christ." There is a translational explanation that Paul's confident and unhindered proclamation of the gospel in Rome forms the climax to the story: "You will be my witnesses in Jerusalem…and to the ends of the earth." Proclamation supposes more of announcement than telling. This, of course, dates back to the Old Testament when Isaiah stated, "To proclaim liberty to the captives; release to the prisoners; To announce a year of favor from the Lord" (Isa. 61:1–2). It also manifests God's purpose for everyone, which includes our lives welded with those around us—at home, school, work, and society in general is all-embracing. "But I have raised you up for this purpose, that I might show you my power and that my name might be proclaimed in all the earth" (Exod. 9:16).

The big picture drawn from both the Old and the New Testaments should be captured as a hybrid of the two words—*witness* and *announce*. Leaders and teachers are placed here to be at the forefront to carry out the assignment. How do we proclaim? By our deed and word and in the way we live our lives, showing how we imitate Christ Jesus's way of life while on earth. By our fruit, we are expected to depict the gospel message. Proclaiming is therefore a combination of our teaching formally as well as informally, drawing the converts to Christ by sharing the gospel through meeting the physical and spiritual needs of those we proclaim to. We must thus know and accept that Jesus is the Savior and Lord who will come to judge the world and reign as king.

Love

The glue that will be needed to put all together for the smooth functioning of the system will now come to play to ensure a perfect harmony as given: "And above all of these put on love which binds everything together in perfect harmony. And let the peace of Christ rule in your hearts, to which indeed you were called one body. And be thankful. Let the word of Christ dwell in you richly. Teaching and admonishing one another in all wisdom, singing psalms and hymns and spiritual songs, with thankfulness in your hearts to God" (Col. 3:14–16 ESV). This is also shown with repetitive imagery in 1 Corinthians: "If I speak in the tongues of men and of angels, but have no love, I am a noisy gong or clamping cymbal. And if I have prophetic powers, but have not love, I am nothing. If I give away all I have and if I deliver up my body to be burned, but have not love, I gain nothing. Love is patient and kind; love does not envy or boast; it is not irritable. It does not insist on its own way; it is not irritable or resentful" (1Cor. 13:2–13 ESV).

When speaking of love, there is the tendency to switch into faith and hope as they constitute a sort of triad in the Christian life and are interrelated as well as fundamental. The greatest of these, we are taught, is love because it remains if and when the other features yield to life's circumstances. In leading and teaching, love, as we have noted above, sustains the teacher/learner relationship and actually oils the engine of modeling and mentoring. In the bigger picture, Christ Himself provided a broader scope in His illustration about "who is your neighbor." He left adequate room to accommodate the need to incorporate love in every effort at making disciples for Christ. Love clearly serves as the invisible "chain-link" constantly applied in different settings to reinforce and strengthen God's purpose, such as the father's love poured out in the father's forgiveness to the prodigal son, and for certain, God's own show of benevolent love, manifested by letting His only begotten Son shed His life for us while we were all still sinners.

The one simple way of demonstrating our reciprocal love for Him remains our commitment in keeping His commands and loving our neighbor. If we cannot put into practice the love of our mentee (neighbor) in our leadership activities, which embodies teaching, then there must be a serious flaw in our performance. The chain continues to elongate to include love of Christ's body, the church, also known as the family of God, and even our enemies by our seeking what is best for them, realizing that it mirrors God's love to a lost world. We love because He first loved us (John 4:19). It is on this basis that we are encouraged as leaders/teachers to continue to strengthen and extend the chain until we are all one in Christ. Christian education seals it with the concept that true love is part of God's nature, and God is the source of love. In spite of our flawed and often corrupted understanding of love, we are called to follow the examples

Christ showed while here on earth and the instructions to our leaders/teachers whose qualifications are explicitly made known to us in Scriptures.

The concept of love under reference here is completely at odds with the meaning ascribed to it in the present generation or, indeed, society. You will often hear phraseology from corporate leaders who would admit, "I can use him in the raw materials handling department" when asked to confirm the existence of a vacancy for a new hire. No consideration is ever given to human relationship whether at time of hire or while on the job. Community intra-relatedness certainly plays no part in most groups you are likely to come across. Biblically-oriented leaders do understand the value for authentic relationship with those they lead or work with. As Paul puts it: "Having so fond an affection for you, we were well-pleased to impart to you not only the gospel of God but also our own lives, because you had become very dear to us" (1 Thess. 2:8) You can discern the color and feel of love from this utterance. Ayers propounds it as: "Community breathes life into leadership and grounds it in the supreme moral virtue that must accompany all truly biblical leaders—namely agape Love." In light of this, he then defines biblical leadership to be: "A biblical leader is a person of character and competence who influences a community of people to achieve a God-honoring calling by means of the power of Christ."[85] This falls in sync with the covenant of teaching which the leader will always be conscious not to work outside of, namely: I have knowledge of something, and you would like to learn about that, or someone else feels you should learn about this, and so lets both of us to try to work together to help you learn about it. That leads automatically not to a unidirectional flow, but to two agents who together share responsibility for the outcome of combined interests. We are here again drawn to the practical approach of not detaching teaching from leadership because the latter is incomplete without the skills of the former.

SELF-REFLECTION

The society in which we live today has suffered several revolutions of different magnitudes, which have been defined according to the impact they have made on human life. These include industrial, religious, educational, and so forth, but the social/moral revolution has not had the privilege of being appropriately identified and named. Technology has been misused to negatively impact the original societal base, namely, the family, our first teaching and learning environment. Any discourse regarding the family in our present dispensation tends to sound more like a historical or simply a textbook prescription for living. It is even sometimes difficult nowadays to get an audience to have a clear image of what constitutes a family. The new thing or notion of "my private space" and the effort to protect it has further eroded the once-formidable unit and foundation of society, which now appears to be struggling to survive.

The notion of family as a unit of human association and relationship no longer fosters unity with the new reality. You can easily test this by paying a visit to what you may consider to be an average family. You will most likely discover that each member in the household is busy in his or her own corner (space), clicking away on his laptop or tablet or on the phone or game station, while the other is watching a TV program. There is hardly any conversation among and within members. No time gets allotted to eating together nor reasoning together or even praying together. When they do occasionally assemble as a family, there is hardly any conversation since a brother would simply text his sibling sitting on the next couch whatever message he wants to convey. What purpose would any conversation serve? Parental control is limited to the point at which being mindful of encroachment into "personal space" is observed.

What the Bible instructed with regard to how parents should transmit knowledge down to the children is now perceived as ancient biblical history. This new subculture has gradually encroached into the school environment, putting teachers in a fairly awkward position such that she has to mind her words, actions, interactions, reactions, and even body language to avoid being accused of some variation of "inappropriate" behavior. Far into the general society, the situation has magnified to the point that everyone is literally forced to operate with delicate maneuvers to avoid offending the next person.

In the heat generated by this new culture, issues such as leadership and teaching are seemingly firmly separated in order to deal appropriately with set goals while avoiding conflict of interest. Detachment of teaching from leadership is seen to allow and promote better room for appreciation of the importance of each office or profession. Practices as seen in today's reality justify such separation; hence it may not even make sense to the present generation if asked to perceive one as an element of the other. It is treated purely as textbook material and at best, an academic construct. And of course concepts like love took a dramatic change in meaning and definition. The agape love ideas no longer have a place in ordinary discourse but are consigned to the dustbins of history or textbook topics that dealt along with wilderness lessons drawn from Moses and his inability to reach the Promised Land.

Christian education is faced with this cloud, which continues to get darker by the day, thus making it difficult to forge relationships inherent in human affairs for the purpose of man's transformation to salvation. The culture of communal living and mind-set, which was practiced in the time of Christ on earth has been completely eroded such that it cannot even be imagined by today's generation. The present club mentality does not come anywhere close to help understand and assimilate the biblical sense, which is the basis of the commission to love one another. If the family relationship is broken beyond repair, love, the spiritual glue, can certainly not perform in the circumstance. The dot-com age no longer permits or allow for dialogue. The WiFi and Zoom age is occupied by a search for real-time audio/video conferencing and the online banking and shopping sessions that make for efficiency rather than human conversation and relationship. Love of one another has no place to function in this kind of environment. Leadership and teaching, separated or not, are pushed out of the setting. However, it is argued here that diminishing their importance does not and cannot alter their congruency.

CONCLUSION

Most writers agree that there is a crisis in the definition of leadership, and a few like Warren Bennis and Burt Nanus have openly cried out about the topic of leadership as representing one of the social sciences' greatest disappointments:

Decades of academic analysis have given us more than 850 definitions of leadership. Literally thousands of empirical investigations of leaders have been conducted in the last seventy-five years alone, but no clear and unequivocal understanding exists as to what distinguishes leaders from non-leaders, and perhaps more important, what distinguishes effective leaders from ineffective leaders and effective organizations from ineffective organizations. Never have so many labored so long to say so little. Multiple interpretations of leadership exist, each providing a silver insight but each remaining an incomplete and wholly inadequate explanation.[86]

They join the chorus of other social scientists/theorists who have lost faith in traditional conceptions of leadership and others who made a strong case for character formation in the process of teaching but made little or no reference to the Bible, the source of authority from which Christian education draws its teaching principles. There are, however, some who have continued to push for a return to the Christian foundation and to resurrect the Christocentric sense of purpose now conflicted with visioning. New constructs are devised with the use of new language, catch phrases, and social practices that help to disconnect teaching from leadership, thus distancing it from our way of life. Alan A. Block succinctly expresses it in his *Ethics and Teaching*: "I wonder if I am educating my students to teach or to practice. If the former, I teach a craft but if the latter, I offer a vision, an art, a way of life."[87] There is equally no generally accepted format for evaluating teachers who are ultimately charged to recreate their students. The culture of fragmentation has eaten so deep into our life style that one hardly realizes that a path that enables us to reason together as a whole is more rewarding than one that places primacy on the parts. And it is a surer way to a sustainable society, which we all aspire to having. Anything to the contrary leads to perpetual fermentation. Put together, all contribute to unstable leadership definitions and practices. This book has merely scratched the surface of what needs to be done to raise awareness to the fact that *teaching is an essential element of leadership.*

RECOMMENDATIONS

1. Christian education should champion the redefinition of leadership in line with the biblical foundational meaning in order to guide society toward a whole-man transformational growth, along with spiritual maturity, and stop the drift away from God's purpose for which leaders are nurtured.

2. Since all truth is God's truth, the detachment of teaching from the concept of leadership is a clear misrepresentation of the commission we all, as believers, are given. A rethink is absolutely needed in order to foster the link with which teaching is associated with leadership. Every leadership training must highlight teaching *as an essential element.*

3. Additional investigation is required to correct the disunity of purpose and accelerate the push for a commonality in understanding of what leadership ought to be. The excuse that several variables have made it impossible to agree on a common meaning is unsustainable if we reconcile our sense of purpose.

NOTES

1. Lawrence O. Richards, *Jesus Christ.* Zondervan (1975) p. 310 *Christian Education: Seeking to Become Like* Publishing House, Grand Rapids, Michigan

2. Pope Paul VI. *Gravissimum Educationis* (Declaration on Christian education). Apostolic Exhortations (October 25, 1965) Paragraph #2

3. Max Depree, *Leadership Is an Art*, Dell Publishing. New York (1989) p. 11

4. Ibid., p. 33

5. Ibid., p. 148

6. Ibid., p. 131–132

7. Tom Barrett, *Dare to Dream and to Win*, Business/Life Management Inc. Vienna, Virginia (1998) p. 145

8. Jay Parini; *The Art of Teaching*, Oxford University Press Inc. New York (2005) p. 59

9. Richards, *Christian Education*, p. 315

10. Abraham Zaleznik, "Managers and Leaders: Are they Different?" *Harvard Business Review*, Harvard Business School Press, Boston Mass 02163 (1998) p. 76

11. Ibid., p. 78

12. Ibid., p. 80

13. John F McArthur, *Called to Lead*, Thomas Nelson Publishers (2004) p.4

14. Albert R Mohler, *The Conviction to Lead*, Bethany House Publishers. Bloomington, MN 55438 (2012) p. 15

15. Philip Seleznick, *Leadership in Administration*, University of California Press (1984) p. 22

16. Urban Meyer and Wayne Coffey; *Above the Line*, Penguin Press, New York (2015) p. 1

17. Ibid., p. 37

18. Ibid., p. 201

19. Ibid., p. 222

20. Firehouse; 8 Essential Elements of Leadership, (www.firehouse.com) Accessed 7/15/2019.

21. Ronald A. Heifetz, Leadership without Easy Answers by (1995) Scott London Article Review, www.scottlondon.com/reviews/heifetz.html Accessed on 7/02/2019.

22. Ibid.

23. Philip Seleznick; *Leadership in Administration*, p. 25

24. Peter Senge; *The Fifth Discipline: Art and Practice of a Learning Organization*, Doubleday, New York (2006) p. 4

25. Ibid., worldcat.org/editorial review/Publisher/Synopsis

26. Peter Senge, The Fifth Discipline: The Art and Practice of the learning Organization, Doubleday, New York (2006) p.12

27. Lois E. LeBar; *Education That Is Christian*, David C Cook, Colorado Springs, Colorado (1995) p. 289

28. Ibid. p. 291

29. Jay Parini; *The Art of Teaching*, Oxford University press, New York (2005) p. 105

30. Ibid. p. 59

31. Bill Smoot, *Conversation with Diverse Group of Teachers*, Indiana University Press, Bloomington, Indiana (2010) p. 68

32. Jay Parini, *The Art of Teaching*, Oxford University Press, New York (2005) p. 105

33. Smoot and Hanna Bowles, *Conversation with Diverse Group of Teachers*, Indiana University Press, Bloomington, Indiana (2010) p. 239

34. Steven Farr, Teaching as Leadership: The highly effective teacher, Josey-Bass a Wiley imprint, 989 market St. San Francisco 94103 (2010) p. xiii

35. Ibid.

36. Max DePree, *Leadership Is an Art*, Dell Publishing Group, Inc. New York (1989) p. 33

37. Teach For America (TFA) Editorial (www.teachforamerica.org/leadership) July 2018 Accessed 06/15/2019

38. Arne Duncan, Teach to Lead: Advancing Teacher Leadership- Remarks of U.S. Secretary of Education, (March 14, 2014) www.press@ed.gov.

39. Ibid., p. 3

40. Ibid., p. 4

41. Ibid., p. 4

42. Ibid., p. 6

43. Smoot and Hanna Bowles, Conversation with Great Teachers, Indiana University Press, (2010) p. 239

44. R. B. Zuck; *Teaching as Jesus Taught*, Grand Rapids, Baker (1995) p. 17

45. Vanessa Rodriguez, The Teaching Brain, New Press, 120 Wall Street, New York, N. Y. 10005 (2014) P. xi

46. Stanley McChrystal, Jeff Eggers, and Jason Mangone, *Leaders: Myth and Reality*, Portfolio/Penguin Publishers, New York, (2018) p. 7–9

47. Joseph S. Nye Jr., Oxford University Press. 198 Madison Ave. New York, N. Y. (2008) p. x-xi

48. Lorenzo Cherubini, Grounded Analysis Theory-An extract published in *International Journal of Teachers Leadership*, Vol. 1, No.1. (Winter, 2008 edition.)

49. Marilyn Kutzenmeyer, Awakening the Sleeping Giant: Helping Teachers Develop as Leaders, Corwin, a Sage company, 2455 Teller Rd., Thousand Oaks, California 91320 (2009) p. 5

50. Teach to Lead Vision Statement, (www.Teachtolead.org/vision)

51. Ibid.

52. Brad Lomenick, *The Catalyst Leader: 8 Essentials for Becoming a Change Maker*, Thomas Nelson Publishing Inc. Nashville, Tennessee (2013) p. xxxii

53. Ibid. p. 219–233

54. Ashira Prossack, Forbes Women, URL:https://www.forbes.com/ashiraprossack1/2018/07/31 Accessed on 06/15/2019.

55. Brad Lomenick, *The Catalyst Leader*, 8 Essentials for Becoming a Change Maker, Thomas Nelson Publishing Inc. Nashville, Tennessee p.211

56. Ibid. p. xvi

57. Karen B. Tye, *Basics of Christian Education*, Chalice Press, Danvers, Massachusetts (2000) p. 127

58. Pope John Paul II, *Familiaris Consortio* (The Role of Christian Family in the modern world). Apostolic Exhortations (November 22, 1981). Paragraph # 21

59. Mike Ayers, *5 Distinctives of Biblical Leadership*, https://ftc.com/resourcelibrary/blog-entries(2016) Accessed on 06/17/2019.

60. Brad Lomenick, The Catalyst Leader, Thomas Nelson Pub. Inc. Nashville Tenn. (2013) p.22

61. Ibid. p30-31

62. Christie Caine, www.austinburkhart.com/core-authenticity (Accessed 9/01/19)

63. Brad Lomenick, The Catalyst Leader, Thomas Nelson Pub. Inc. Nashville Tenn. (2013) p.153 P. 153

64. Ibid. p. 213

65. Zygmunt Bauman, Review Article by Keith Tester- Contemporary Sociology by American Sociological Assn. Vol.31, No. 4 (July 2002) pp. 442 and 443

66. Merriam-Webster Dictionary, 11th. Edition

67. David M Chavis & David W. McMillan, Journal of Community Psychology Vol.14. (January 1986)

68. James R. Estep Jr., Michael Anthony, and Gregg R. Alison, *Theology for Christian Education*, B & H Publishing Group, Nashville Tennessee (2008) p. 115

69. Ibid. p.225

70. Lawrence O. Richards, Christian Education: Seeking to Become Like Jesus, Zondervan Publishing House, Grand Rapid, Michigan ((1975) p. 213

71. Max Bergholz, Imagined Communities: Reflections on the Origins and Spread of Nationalism by Benedict Anderson, Reviewed in The American Historical Review, Vol. 123 (March 2018)

72. Benedict Anderson, Imagined communities: Reflections on the Origin and Spread of Nationalism, Verso Publishers, 180 Varick Street, New York, N. Y. 10014 (2006) p. 6

73. Abner Cohen, Two-dimensional man: An essay on the anthropology of power and symbolism in complex society, Routledge Publishers, 711 Third Ave. New York, N.Y. 10017, (1976) Routledge Library ed. p.4

74. Chris Arnade, Dignity, Sentinel Penguin, Random House, New York (2019) p. 47

75. Ibid. p. 82

76. Graham Day, Community and Everyday Life, A review by Marian Cadogan –article in Sociology Volume 41, No. 4 (August 1,2007) p. 750-752

77. Chris Arnade, Dignity, Sentinel Penguin Pub. Random House (2019) p.45-46

78. Jeff Sharlet, The Family, Harper Collins Publishers, New York (2008) p.314

79. Ron Brandt, On Rethinking Leadership: A Conversation with Tom Segiovanni, Educational Leadership Journal, February 1992 Vol. 49 No. 5

80. Lawrence Richards, Christian Education; Seeking to become Like Jesus Christ, Zondervan Publishing House, Grand Rapids, Michigan (1975) p. 81

81. Mike Ayers, 5 Distinctives of Biblical Leadership, www.ftc.com/resourcelibrary/blogentries Accessed 06/15/2019

82. Lawrence O. Richards, Christian Education, Zondervan Publishing House, Grand Rapids, Michigan (1975) p. 242

83. Ibid. p.54

84. Ibid. p. 287

85. Mike Ayers, 5 Distinctives of Biblical Leadership, (www.ftc.com/resourcelibrary/blog-entries) Accessed 06/15/2019

86. Warren Bennis and Burt Nanus, Leaders: Strategy for Taking Charge, Harper Business Essentials 2nd. Edition, Harper Collins Publishers, N.Y. (2003) p. 4
87. Alan A. Block, *Ethics and Teaching*, Palgrave Macmillan, New York (2009) p. 29

BIBLIOGRAPHY

1. Lawrence O. Richards, *Jesus Christ.* Zondervan (1975) p. 310 *Christian Education: Seeking to Become Like* Publishing House, Grand Rapids, Michigan

2. Pope Paul VI. *Gravissimum Educationis* (Declaration on Christian education). Apostolic Exhortations (October 25, 1965) Paragraph #2

3. Max Depree, *Leadership Is an Art*, Dell Publishing. New York (1989) p. 11

4. Ibid., p. 33

5. Ibid., p. 148

6. Ibid., p. 131–132

7. Tom Barrett, *Dare to Dream and to Win*, Business/Life Management Inc. Vienna, Virginia (1998) p. 145

8. Jay Parini; *The Art of Teaching*, Oxford University Press Inc. New York (2005) p. 59

9. Richards, *Christian Education*, p. 315

10. Abraham Zaleznik, "Managers and Leaders: Are they Different?" *Harvard Business Review*, Harvard Business School Press, Boston Mass 02163 (1998) p. 76

11. Ibid., p. 78

12. Ibid., p. 80

13. John F McArthur, *Called to Lead*, Thomas Nelson Publishers (2004) p.4

14. Albert R Mohler, *The Conviction to Lead*, Bethany House Publishers. Bloomington, MN 55438 (2012) p. 15

15. Philip Seleznick, *Leadership in Administration*, University of California Press (1984) p. 22

16. Urban Meyer and Wayne Coffey; *Above the Line*, Penguin Press, New York (2015) p. 1

17. Ibid., p. 37

18. Ibid., p. 201

19. Ibid., p. 222

20. Firehouse; 8 Essential Elements of Leadership, www.firehouse.com Accessed 7/15/2019.

21. Ronald A. Heifetz, Leadership without Easy Answers by (1995) Scott London Article Review, www.scottlondon.com/reviews/heifetz.html Accessed on 7/02/2019.

22. Ibid.

23. Philip Seleznick; *Leadership in Administration*, p. 25

24. Peter Senge; *The Fifth Discipline: Art and Practice of a Learning Organization*, Doubleday, New York (2006) p. 4

25. Ibid., worldcat.org/editorial review/Publisher/Synopsis

26. Peter Senge, The Fifth Discipline: The Art and Practice of the learning Organization, Doubleday, New York (2006) p.12

27. Lois E. LeBar; *Education That Is Christian*, David C Cook, Colorado Springs, Colorado (1995) p. 289

28. Ibid., p. 291

29. Jay Parini; *The Art of Teaching*, Oxford University press, New York (2005) p. 105

30. Ibid., p. 59

31. Bill Smoot, *Conversation with Diverse Group of Teachers*, Indiana University Press, Bloomington, Indiana (2010) p. 68

32. Jay Parini, *The Art of Teaching*, Oxford university Press, New York (2005) p. 105

33. Smoot and Hanna Bowles, *Conversation with Diverse Group of Teachers*, Indiana University Press, Bloomington, Indiana (2010) p. 239

34. Steven Farr, Teaching as Leadership: The highly effective teacher, Josey-Bass a Wiley imprint, 989 market St. San Francisco 94103 (2010) p. xiii

35. Ibid.

36. Max DePree, *Leadership Is an Art*, Dell Publishing Group, Inc. New York (1989) p. 33

37. Teach For America (TFA) Editorial (www.teachforamerica.org/leadership) July 2018 Accessed 06/15/2019

38. Arne Duncan, Teach to Lead: Advancing Teacher Leadership- Remarks of U.S. Secretary of Education, (March 14, 2014) www.press@ed.gov.

39. Ibid., p. 3

40. Ibid., p. 4

41. Ibid., p. 4

42. Ibid., p. 6

43. Smoot and Hanna Bowles, Conversation with Great Teachers, Indiana University Press, (2010) p. 239

44. R. B. Zuck; *Teaching as Jesus Taught*, Grand Rapids, Baker (1995) p. 17

45. Vanessa Rodriguez, The Teaching Brain, New Press, 120 Wall Street, New York, N. Y. 10005 (2014) p. xi

46. Stanley McChrystal, Jeff Eggers, and Jason Mangone, *Leaders: Myth and Reality*, Portfolio/Penguin Publishers, New York, (2018) p. 7–9

47. Joseph S. Nye Jr., Oxford University Press. 198 Madison Ave. New York, N. Y. (2008) p. x-xi

48. Lorenzo Cherubini, Grounded Analysis Theory-An extract published in *International Journal of Teachers Leadership*, Vol. 1, No.1. (Winter, 2008 edition.)

49. Marilyn Kutzenmeyer, Awakening the Sleeping Giant: Helping Teachers Develop as Leaders, Corwin, a Sage company, 2455 Teller Rd., Thousand Oaks, California 91320 (2009) p. 5

50. Teach to Lead Vision Statement, (www.Teachtolead.org/vision)

51. Ibid.

52. Brad Lomenick, *The Catalyst Leader: 8 Essentials for Becoming a Change Maker*, Thomas Nelson Publishing Inc. Nashville, Tennessee (2013) p. xxxii

53. Ibid. p. 219–233

54. Ashira Prossack, Forbes Women, URL:https://www.forbes.com/ashiraprossack1/2018/07/31 Accessed on 06/15/2019.

55. Brad Lomenick, *The Catalyst Leader*, 8 Essentials for Becoming a Change Maker, Thomas Nelson Publishing Inc. Nashville, Tennessee p.211

56. Ibid., p. xvi

57. Karen B. Tye, *Basics of Christian Education*, Chalice Press, Danvers, Massachusetts (2000) p. 127

58. Pope John Paul II, *Familiaris Consortio* (The Role of Christian Family in the modern world). Apostolic Exhortations (November 22, 1981). Paragraph # 21

59. Mike Ayers, *5 Distinctives of Biblical Leadership*, https://ftc.com/resourcelibrary/blog-entries (2016) Accessed on 06/17/2019.

60. Brad Lomenick, The Catalyst Leader, Thomas Nelson Pub. Inc. Nashville Tenn. (2013) p.22

61. Ibid. p30-31

62. Christie Caine, (www.austinburkhart.com/core-authenticity) Accessed 9/01/19)

63. Brad Lomenick, The Catalyst Leader, Thomas Nelson Pub. Inc. Nashville Tenn. (2013) P.153 p. 153

64. Ibid. p. 213

65. Zygmunt Bauman, Review Article by Keith Tester-Contemporary Sociology by American Sociological Assn. Vol.31, No. 4 (July 2002) pp. 442 and 443

66. Merriam-Webster Dictionary, 11th. Edition

67. David M Chavis & David W. McMillan, Journal of Community Psychology Vol.14. (January 1986)

68. James R. Estep Jr., Michael Anthony, and Gregg R. Alison, *Theology for Christian Education*, B & H Publishing Group, Nashville Tennessee (2008) p. 115

69. Ibid. p.225

70. Lawrence O. Richards, Christian Education: Seeking to Become Like Jesus, Zondervan Publishing House, Grand Rapid, Michigan ((1975) P. 213

71. Max Bergholz, Imagined Communities: Reflections on the Origins and Spread of Nationalism by Benedict Anderson, Reviewed in The American Historical Review, Vol. 123 (March 2018)

72. Benedict Anderson, Imagined communities: Reflections on the Origin and Spread of Nationalism, Verso Publishers, 180 Varick Street, New York, N. Y. 10014 (2006) p. 6

73. Abner Cohen, Two-dimensional man: An essay on the anthropology of power and symbolism in complex society, Routledge Publishers, 711 Third Ave. New York, N.Y. 10017, (1976) Routledge Library ed. p.4

74. Chris Arnade, Dignity, Sentinel Penguin, Random House, New York (2019) p. 47

75. Ibid. p. 82

76. Graham Day, Community and Everyday Life, A review by Marian Cadogan –article in Sociology Volume 41, No. 4 (August 1,2007) p. 750-752

77. Chris Arnade, Dignity, Sentinel Penguin Pub. Random House (2019) p.45-46

78. Jeff Sharlet, The Family, Harper Collins Publishers, New York (2008) p.314

79. Ron Brandt, On Rethinking Leadership: A Conversation with Tom Segiovanni, Educational Leadership Journal, February 1992 Vol. 49 No. 5

80. Lawrence Richards, Christian Education; Seeking to become Like Jesus Christ, Zondervan Publishing House, Grand Rapids, Michigan (1975) p. 81

81. Mike Ayers, 5 Distinctives of Biblical Leadership, (www.ftc.com/resourcelibrary/blogentries) Accessed 06/15/2019

82. Lawrence O. Richards, Christian Education, Zondervan Publishing House, Grand Rapids, Michigan (1975) p. 242

83. Ibid. p.54

84. Ibid. p. 287

85. Mike Ayers, 5 Distinctives of Biblical Leadership, www.ftc.com/resourcelibrary/blogentries   Accessed 06/15/2019

86. Warren Bennis and Burt Nanus, Leaders: Strategy for Taking Charge, Harper Business Essentials 2nd. Edition, Harper Collins Publishers, N.Y. (2003) p. 4

87. Alan A. Block, *Ethics and Teaching*, Palgrave Macmillan, New York (2009) p. 29

88. All Bible references are from NIV except those indicated otherwise e.g. NARE-New American Revised Edition.

Other Sources Consulted

1. Brandt, Ron, "On Rethinking Leadership: A Conversation with Tom Segiovanni," *Educational Leadership Journal*, February 1992, Vol. 49, Number 5.

2. Chang, Deborah, (online contributor) 9 Reasons Great Teachers make Great Leaders, https://www. huffingtonpost.com. Deborah-Chang/9-reasons-great-teachers. Accessed on 06/25/2019

3. Lorenzo Cherubini, "Grounded Analysis Theory," *International Journal of Teachers Leadership*, vol.1, No.1 Winter 2008 edition.

4. Davies, Mervyn and Graham Dobbs, *Leadership in the Church for a People of Hope*, T and T Clark International, New York (2011)

5. Farr, Steven, *Teaching as Leadership: The Highly Effective Teacher*, Josey-Bass, San Francisco (2010). p. xiii

6. Ibid., p. 5.

7. Kutzenmeyer, Marilyn, *Awakening the Sleeping Giant: Helping Teachers Develop as Leaders*, Corwin, Thousand Oaks, CA (2009). p.5

8. Lomenick, *The Catalyst*. p. xvi Rodriguez, Vanessa, *The Teaching Brain*, New Press, New York (2014). p. xi, 4

9. Ibid., p. xvi, xviii

10. Matthew Kelly, *Rediscover Jesus*, Beacon Publishing Erlanger KY (2015). p. 67

11. Maxwell, John, *Irrefutable Laws of Leadership*, Thomas Nelson Publishers, Nashville, TN (1998)

12. Mervyn, Davis and Dobbs, Graham, *Leadership in the Church for a People of Hope*, T and T Clark International 80 Maiden Ln., Suit 704 New York, N.Y. 10038 (2011)

13. Nye, Joseph S. Jr., *The Powers to Lead*, Oxford University Press, New York, (2008) Preface, Ch. 5

14. Pazmino, Robert W., *Foundational Issues in Christian Education*, 3rd edition, Grand Rapids, Baker (2008). p. 53

15. Pitirim A.Sorokin, Society Culture and Personality, Harper & Brown Publishers, New York (1947) p.243

16. Richards, *Christian Education*. p. 54

17. Ibid., p. 134

18. Ibid., p. 140

19. Rodriguez, Vanessa, *The Teaching Brain*, New Press, New York, (2014). p. xi, 4

20. Staw, Barry M. and Salancik, Gerald R. eds., *New Directions in Organizational Behavior*, Chicago: St. Clair (1977), p. 182

21. Yount, William R., *Called to Teach: An introduction to the Ministry of Teaching*, Nashville, B and H (1999)

22. Other sites visited on the internet:

    a. Andrea Breazeale, Elements of Leadership (www.breazealeeaa.com(2014)) Accessed 5/23/2019;

    b. Steven Anderson, Integrated Leadership Systems (www.integratedleader.com/key elements/lead) Accessed 6/30/2019

c. What does the Bible say? (<u>www.gotquestion.org/ Bible-teaching-html</u>) Accessed 5/23/2019

d. Jesus Film Project, Making Disciples, (<u>www.jesusfilm. org/blog/disciple-making</u>) Accessed 5/25/2019

e. God's Purpose (<u>www.whatchristianswanttoknow. com/important-bible-verses</u>) Accessed 6/01/2019

f. Dr. Willis Newman-Bible Teaching, (<u>www.bible teaching-about-leadership/christianleadership</u>) Accessed 1/29/2019